Prayer Group Workshop

Edited by
Bert Ghezzi and John Blattner

SERVANT BOOKS
Ann Arbor, Michigan

All of the articles collected in this book have previously
appeared in *New Covenant* magazine. "Who Can We
Help?" by Gabe Meyer, was originally published in the
February 1977 issue of *Pastoral Renewal*, copyright © 1977
by *Pastoral Renewal*. "A Change of Heart or a Change of
Leaders?" by Kevin Perrotta, was originally published in the
August 1978 issue of *Pastoral Renewal;* copyright © 1978 by
Pastoral Renewal. "The New Temple," by Gerry Rauch,
originally appeared in the March-April 1978 issue of the
ICO Newsletter.

Printed in the United States of America

ISBN 0-89283-066-2

Contents

INTRODUCTION

The prayer group is one of the basic components of the Catholic charismatic renewal. For many of the million or so individuals around the world who identify themselves as "members" of the charismatic renewal, belonging to the renewal generally means participating in a prayer group.

Prayer groups are deceptively difficult to define. Some are explicitly oriented to a particular parish; some include members of many parishes; some meet in living rooms and don't think of themselves as parish organizations at all. Most have fewer than fifty members, though many are larger. Most are predominantly Catholic, though many are explicitly ecumenical. Some groups function on the basis of fairly clearly defined commitments, but in most cases the "prayer group" is simply that group of people who show up more or less regularly for the weekly prayer meeting.

Despite the fact that nothing like an official "order of service" has ever been formulated in the charismatic renewal, prayer meetings around the world display a remarkable similarity in structure and format. A participant in the charismatic renewal can visit almost any prayer meeting, anywhere, and feel at home. The prayer meeting has become perhaps the primary expression of participation in the renewal.

It is not difficult to understand why this is so. The charismatic renewal is, before all else, a renewal of prayer and praise, both personal and corporate. At the personal level, it features an intimate relationship with the living God. After being baptized in the Holy Spirit, individuals experience a new awareness of God's presence and action in their lives, a stronger urge to pray, a thirst for God's word in Scripture, and a greater desire for personal holiness.

Before long this new life in the Spirit draws together those who have experienced it. By its nature it cannot be an isolated, in-

1

dividual experience. It must be shared. Thus the development of corporate forms of charismatic worship, in the shape of prayer meetings, is the inevitable result of the outpouring of the Spirit, and the growth of prayer groups becomes recognizable as a major action of the Spirit in our day.

As such, prayer groups in the charismatic renewal are important to the whole church. Many groups engage in direct service to their parish or diocese. Even when such avenues of direct corporate service are not open, those individuals whose lives of prayer and service have been nurtured and sustained by prayer groups often make significant contributions. Many parish councils and commissions include among their members people whose dedication to the Lord and his church has been cultivated and strengthened by participation in a prayer group.

Because prayer groups play such a central role in the renewal of the church, it is important that they function well. And it is precisely here that a problem can arise. For all the Holy Spirit's driving force behind the development of prayer groups, a large amount of work and wisdom is required to establish a prayer group and keep it running smoothly. Many have begun by convening a roomful of charismatic "pray-ers" with the idea of simply "letting the Spirit lead" only to find that the Spirit does not seem to operate that way. Rather, he teaches us how to do many of the things that need to be done, and expects us to remember and to apply what we have learned. Most of these lessons concern not deep, mystical truths, but simple, practical ways of doing things.

As might be expected, some groups are more successful at this than others. In fact, for any question that can arise, there probably is some group that has already found an answer. How do you form a music group? What kind of person should lead the prayer group? How do you set up a booktable? What do you do when disagreements erupt?

In a movement as large and diffuse as the charismatic renewal, it isn't easy for groups to find ways to communicate what they've learned with one another. As a result, many prayer groups have tried to answer every question from their own experience. Of course experience is an excellent teacher, but there is a limit to how much "experience" any one prayer group can survive. Groups that can learn from someone else's experience will spare themselves the frustration of making the same mistakes.

That is where this book comes in. In it are short, to-the-point articles on many of the practical aspects of maintaining a prayer group, written by people who have answered some basic questions in their own groups and have seen those answers work. All the authors have had long experience in building successful prayer groups and in helping other groups solve problems and move ahead in serving the Lord. They write specifically to the prayer group situation, from a distinctly "prayer group" perspective.

Each article addresses one basic topic, and lays out a workable approach to that area in a straightforward, often step-by-step, manner. Each is designed so that a prayer group facing a difficulty in a particular area can read the article, make a few adaptations to their unique situation, and implement a solution. Certain topics will apply more readily to some groups than to others — for example, large groups encounter difficulties that small ones do not, and vice-versa. But, each group is likely to find something of value in every article.

My own experience with prayer groups derives from a period of time spent in the Washington, D.C. area, where I was a leader of one prayer group and associated with a number of others. Bert Ghezzi, my coeditor for this book, had long experience building prayer groups in the Grand Rapids, Michigan, area. Our personal familiarity with the needs of prayer groups was a decisive factor in selecting the topics covered in the articles that compose this book.

We owe thanks to Randy Cirner and Jim Manney, who helped us develop this material both as a series in *New Covenant* and as a book, and to Lucy Broad for her patient secretarial help.

John Blattner

I.

Prayer Meetings, Worship, and Music

Saturday night. Folding chairs in concentric circles. Guitarists tuning their instruments. Men and women filter in and find their places, chatting and joking. They grow quiet as the leader moves to the center of the room to announce the opening song.

CHAPTER ONE

EFFECTIVE
PRAYER MEETINGS

John Blattner

A few years ago, just after my wife and I recommitted our lives to the Lord, we began meeting weekly with a small group of Christian friends. We were all new at it, and none of us knew much about how we should spend our time together.

It seemed clear that we should be learning more about Scripture, so we decided to use some of our time for Bible study. We felt it was important to share our lives with one another, so we set aside time for individuals to tell about how things were going in their spiritual lives, answers they'd received to prayers, and so on. We thought it was important that we meet one another's needs, so we made sure we took time to mention our prayer requests and have everybody pray for them.

Since we had all come to the Lord at about the same time, none of us felt comfortable with the thought of being leader of the group. Our discomfort stemmed both from the fact that we felt inexperienced and unqualified, and from a desire to avoid any appearance of conceit.

Although I have pleasant, sentimental recollections of those meetings, I also remember that they were fairly chaotic. We might begin with a time of prayer, only to be interrupted by someone wanting to tell about some experience. After that we'd go back to praying, and before long someone would ask to be prayed over for healing, or would mention a difficult family situation that we should all stop and pray for, or would ask when the Bible study was going to begin, or would suggest that we break for refreshments. It was difficult to concentrate on any one activity, because we were never sure when we might be steered off in a totally new direction.

Without a leader, it wasn't possible for us even to end the meeting on time; often, our fellowships would extend well into the early morning. They ended because they *had* to: everyone was falling asleep. Our Bible studies and discussions went around in circles because no one was in charge of them and we lacked the resources to find answers to even our most basic questions. We were all very sincere in our desire to serve the Lord and one another; we just didn't know much about how to go about it.

Many prayer groups in the charismatic renewal suffer from the same problems that plagued my old fellowship group. A few simple principles can help our prayer meeting to flow more smoothly.

Unless everyone shares a common conception of what should take place at the prayer meeting, confusion is inevitable. The reason we come together in our prayer meetings is to worship and glorify the Lord together, as a group. The focus of a prayer meeting should be *prayer:* all activities, such as sharing experiences, reading Scripture passages, giving teachings, delivering prophecies, and so on, should be directed toward the basic goal of giving glory to God.

Often, other activities can best be conducted outside the prayer meeting. Bible studies, for example, work best when everyone can come prepared to discuss a specific passage, when they've had an opportunity to consult commentaries and other reference aids, and when a qualified leader can be present. That's seldom possible within a prayer meeting. Intercessory prayer is usually handled most effectively in a prayer room after the main meeting, when we can spend enough time to fully understand people's needs and to pray about them adequately and in privacy.

Individuals also need to have the right outlook on their role in the meeting. Many of us approach our weekly prayer meeting with what has been called the "spiritual filling station" mentality: We see it as a place where *our* spiritual needs can be met. We fill our blessing tank on Wednesday night, and then try to make it to the next meeting before we run dry.

This approach shifts our focus from giving to receiving. We have come only to "be fed," when our primary concern should be to serve our brothers and sisters. We should be participants at our prayer meetings, not just spectators.

The weekly prayer meeting is only a part — and a small one — of our spiritual life. We also need to devote time to personal prayer, Scripture study, and regular Christian fellowship. When all the different aspects of our Christian life are functioning properly, we'll be in a position to contribute to our prayer meetings — not just to sit back and expect others to carry the burden alone.

Prayer meetings cannot thrive without structure and leadership. Unless some minimal pattern is followed, it is difficult for people to surrender themselves to what the Spirit is doing. We can be hindered in our praise by the nagging suspicion that, at any moment, we might be unexpectedly directed into a different activity. Or we might have something we want to share with the group, yet not know for sure if and when we will have an opportunity to speak.

Many groups follow a pattern something like this: open with a substantial period of free praise and worship. During this time, praying in tongues, leading the group in spontaneous prayer, singing songs, speaking prophecies, and reading aloud passages from Scripture are all appropriate. Next, invite people to tell about things the Lord has shown them, insights into Scripture, answered prayers, and so on. This can be followed by a talk or prepared sharing (if there is to be one) and — if the group is small enough to do it easily and discreetly — a time of intercessory prayer.

Though it should not be done rigidly or mechanically, using such a pattern can be a freeing experience. We can throw ourselves into worship without worrying about unexpected interruptions. And we can feel confident that we will have an opportunity to share with our brothers and sisters at the appropriate time.

For any pattern or structure to work effectively, it must be coupled with effective leadership. My old prayer meetings would have been vastly improved if one of us had taken responsibility for even the most basic functions: starting and ending on time, moving from one activity to another, and so on.

Of course, a prayer meeting leader's responsibilities go beyond these functional tasks. He or she is not simply a master of ceremonies. In addition to attending to practical matter, the leader should:

— exhort the group to focus its attention on the Lord.

— encourage people to be open to the gifts of the Spirit and to share with the group.

— keep the meeting from going off on a tangent, by gently redirecting accounts of personal experiences, discussions, or other activities that lead the group away from the basic purpose of glorifying God.

— deal with disturbances that arise. This can entail everything from encouraging people not to be distracted by outside noises, to gently but firmly correcting disruptive people.

A man or woman does not have to be a candidate for sainthood in order to lead a prayer meeting. An advanced degree in theology or public speaking, or a dramatic gift of prophecy or healing, is not required. The main requirements are simply a desire to serve the Lord and the group, and an ability to sense and follow the leadings of the Spirit. Some people seem to have a special charism for leading prayer meetings, and that gift shouldn't go unused. We ought not let our fear of spiritual pride lead to a false spiritual humility that prevents us from serving the Lord as he might call us.

In many ways, the key to order and leadership in a prayer meeting rests with the individual members of the group. We should be submissive to, and supportive of, the pattern that has been established. This means that when the group is praying out loud, or singing a song, or worshipping in silence, we do too — not hesitatingly, but with a desire to contribute to the group's wor

ship. It also means following the directions of the leader promptly; this makes it easier for him to help the group respond to the
Holy Spirit.

Sometimes we object to the idea that prayer meetings ought to
have structure and leadership; we fear it will stifle the Holy
Spirit. In fact, the opposite is true: conducting our meetings
"decently and in order" (1 Cor. 14:40, *RSV*) actually frees the
Spirit to move among us in greater power, and it enables us to
respond to the Spirit more readily. Maintaining a clear concept of
the purpose of our prayer meeting, and conducting it with attention to orderliness and leadership, can help our praise and worship flow in the peace and joy of the Spirit.

CHAPTER TWO

SONG, SILENCE,
AND SPONTANEITY

An Interview with Jim Cavnar

Jim Cavnar is familiar to many in the charismatic renewal as music leader at numerous national and international conferences.

Q: What would you say are the distinctive features of worship in the charismatic renewal?

A: I would pick out three elements. They're not entirely new but they're especially prominent.

The first is what is called the "word of prayer." I'll never forget the evening that I first encountered this kind of prayer. A group of us at Notre Dame were invited to the home of Ray Bullard, the president of the local chapter of the Full Gospel Businessmen's Fellowship. Ray had gathered about 20 men from the area to meet with us. Once we were all settled in his basement, Ray said, "Well, let's begin with a word of prayer." What a shock, when everyone in the room simultaneously burst into enthusiastic prayer!

I was accustomed to spontaneous prayer, but nothing like this. I felt like saying, "Wait a minute, I can't tell what you're saying."

Since then, I've come to see that there's a good reason for this kind of prayer. It enables a group to pray together in an active, participative way that builds a spirit of unity and praise. The word of prayer allows for a form of group personal prayer. Each of us speaks individually to God, praying aloud—generally in a moderate tone of voice—so that others can hear that we're praying and are encouraged to pray more fervently themselves.

The second element is song—familiar songs and hymns, spontaneous songs, and singing together in the Spirit. Of course, singing has always been a part of worship, but I think what is different is the degree of spontaneity and participation.

The third element is silence. This seems to be powerful by way of contrast. What I mean is that a period of silence can be an expression of awe and reverence when it occurs spontaneously after a time of vigorous praise and song.

Q: Participation and spontaneity seem to be important in worshipful prayer.

A: Yes, I think participation is significant. Group worship can be more than singing together or having a variety of people say or do various things. We've found the value of having everyone engaged in an active way, seeking after the Lord, expressing their praise, joining wholeheartedly in the songs. People take part in the worship more actively when they're able to contribute to the meeting in other ways—sharing about what God has done for them, speaking the Lord's word, and so on.

I'm convinced that for there to be effective worship this element of full involvement needs to be encouraged and developed.

Worshipful prayer also needs spontaneity. Which songs we choose, whether we pray aloud or silently, whether we stand and shout and clap or sit down and pray meditatively is based on our immediate sense of what will draw us closer to God—what we need to do to respond to God's presence with us.

Worshipful prayer thrives where there is an expectation of God speaking to us, changing us, leading us to respond to him in different ways. Worship becomes a way of responding to what he is doing now.

I would also add a third characteristic for worshipful prayer.

That is a kind of unity or "flow." This is difficult to describe. I mean that one aspect of worship leads to another; each part evolves naturally from what has gone before. There is no disruption. The prayer is not disjointed, but everything fits into an organic whole.

Q: What can leaders do to help people move toward more participation, spontaneity, and unity in worship?

A: Basically, we have to bring people to a conscious openness to the action of the Holy Spirit in their lives. But this isn't enough in itself.

One thing I learned some years ago when I first began to lead prayer meetings in the charismatic renewal is that there are few groups of people who will naturally enter into worshipful prayer in the way I've been describing it. There generally needs to be a considerable amount of teaching and leading and learning from experience.

The group of leaders has to work together to make worshipful prayer a central part of the service or meeting. Personal sharing, readings from Scripture, teaching, or singing ought to complement worshipful prayer, but too often they displace simple adoration from the central position it ought to have.

The person who leads the worship needs to be working with whoever is in charge of the music. I suggest there be a regular time for these people to communicate with one another and develop a common approach.

People must be taught how to worship. One of the things that people have the greatest difficulty doing is giving their whole hearts and attention to the Lord himself and not being distracted by their needs, by the desire to tell people about something that happened in their lives, and so on. At the beginning it requires repeated instruction and exhortation in order for people to put aside distraction and seek after the Lord in prayer for any period of time.

People need to be taught that we shouldn't allow ourselves to be held back from worshipping God because we don't feel like it. Worshipful prayer is similar to love. We must love one another whether we feel like it or not; that is, we lay down our lives for one another. Likewise, we worship God because of who God is, not because of the feelings we have.

We ought to help people see that the goal in worship is to bring ourselves into contact with God in order that we may love him and be totally given to him. Our goal is to put God first so that he is glorified and we come to know him as God.

Q: What helps people enter into worshipful prayer?

A: Being conscious of the reality of God and attentive to seeking him. The leader of the worship service can assist people in doing this.

He can introduce a period of worshipful prayer with an exhortation focusing everyone on the Lord. Personal testimonies and preaching about the Lord can give people a sense of God's reality and presence. Often the most natural thing to do after preaching is to lead people in a period of worship.

There are times when we need to simply be quiet and stop the ceaseless flow of our own ideas and thoughts and wait for God. Then he begins to speak or work, leading us to a particular song or to a particular way of praying.

Q: What principles do you use in choosing music for worship?

A: There are a lot of songs that are fun to sing or are esthetically pleasing but are not very effective in enabling a group to worship God. There may be other songs that seem too utterly simple or don't seem great from a musical point of view but have a tremendous power to help us in worship. So our musical preferences should inform us somewhat, but we should be careful not to let them limit us.

I would say that the only way to find out if a particular song is good for worship is to try it out and have the experience of the song.

Q: If the criterion is what you experience when you sing a song, how do you distinguish between something that's helping you

*pray and something that's simply evoking some kind of feeling?
Many churches have been plagued with music that's overly sentimental.*

A: We need to choose songs not because they evoke feelings but
because they enable us to express something to God that it's right
and healthy to express — they're songs that enable us to experience
the Lord as God, not just to experience our own nice feelings.

There is clearly a matter of spiritual discernment that goes into
selecting songs. If the songs are overly sentimental and display an
excessive affectation, they will cultivate a spirituality in the group
that's overly sentimental. If the songs express strength, endurance, and rejoicing, they will teach strength, endurance, and rejoicing.

*Q: What effects does worshipful prayer have on a group of Chris-
tians?*

A: For individuals, it brings them into a stronger relationship
with God, orienting their lives toward God himself, toward an
obedience to God, toward seeking after God. For a group as a
whole, it awakens the gifts of the Spirit, because we are brought
into a closer contact with God, opened up to God. We are much
more receptive to the power of the Spirit.

Also, I think a body of people who have united in worshipful
prayer of God invariably experience a lot of guidance from him
because worship brings them into contact with God and he can
speak to them more clearly.

*Q: Would you comment on the approach to worship and
thanksgiving that is oriented around our needs?*

A: There has been an emphasis of late that praise is important in
our being receptive to God's working in our lives. This is very
true. But if it becomes a mechanism for getting God to act, it
ceases to be an authentic form of worship. Worship has to be
something that's oriented toward God for his sake, not a tool for
getting God to answer our prayers.

CHAPTER THREE

LEARNING TO WORSHIP

David Podegracz

Y ET an hour is coming, and is already here, when authentic worshipers will worship the Father in Spirit and truth. Indeed, it is just such worshipers the Father seeks. God is Spirit, and those who worship him must worship in Spirit and truth" (John 4:23-24, *NAB*).

Worship is not something that just happens. We need to work at it, just as we work at other basic elements of the Christian life.

There are several different ways that God's people worship and praise him:

1. *The word of praise* — giving glory to God, as the psalmist does in psalms 100 and 150.

2. *The festal shout* — an acclamation of the Lord which celebrates his deeds among us (a contemporary example is the "3-2-1-Glory!" shout made popular by Bobbie Cavnar).

3. *Expressing thanks* — a time when individuals stand up and spontaneously thank God for various things.

4. *Inspired song and plain singing* — inspired song is a spontaneous song which draws those assembled into deep praise. Plain singing refers to songs sung by the entire assembly to praise God.

5. *Singing in the Spirit* — spontaneous melodies which emerge from the whole group, usually sung in tongues.

6. *Dancing before the Lord* — to dance out of appreciation for the opportunity to praise God.

How does a group grow in praise?

In order to effectively lead a group in praise and worship, two key elements should be present: a good leader and a responsive, cooperative music group.

A good leader is one who can guide a group into worship, and help people respond to the Spirit without stopping the worship or drawing attention to himself.

In most cases, a prayer meeting leader should not lead the music. A division of labor between the leader of the prayer meeting and the leader of the music allows everything to run more smoothly. While the prayer meeting leader concentrates on the meeting as a whole, the music leader concerns himself with thinking of appropriate and helpful songs.

A music leader who is responsive and cooperative is equal in importance to the prayer meeting leader himself. He must follow the prayer meeting leader's directions at all times. Part of the responsibility of a prayer meeting leader is to lead the music, and the music leader is to be obedient to his direction. If, for example, the prayer meeting leader asks for a slow, worshipful song, the music leader should be obedient to his direction, even if he thinks another type of song would be more appropriate.

Often, of course, it will be a major part of the music leader's service to take the initiative in selecting songs for use in the prayer meeting, though he checks with the prayer meeting leader before proceeding.

There are several specific areas that we can concentrate on in learning how to worship more effectively.

1. *Perseverance.* To praise with perseverance may involve devoting more time to praising God than we're used to — perhaps spending 20 to 30 minutes of our prayer meetings doing nothing but praising God.

Perseverance is especially effective in breaking through feelings and attitudes which block our worship. Tiredness, discouragement, and anxiety make it difficult for us to focus our attention on the Lord. When such feelings and attitudes prevail in our meetings, devoting a good deal of time to worship can enable us to open our hearts to receiving the Lord's word.

2. *Singing*. Much of our growth in praise depends on the songs we sing and how we sing them. We need to learn which songs are appropriate for leading people into praise and sustaining it.

3. *Directions*. To direct the group's worship effectively, the prayer meeting leader needs to spend time preparing for the meetings, seeking the Lord's will, establishing good relationships with group members. He should be able to encourage, correct, and exhort the group. Above all, he must learn to be sensitive to the Holy Spirit.

Group members need to be obedient to the direction they receive. A prayer group cannot grow in praise unless the leader is free to guide and direct the meetings.

4. *Word Gifts*. Preaching, prophecy, exhortation, inspired prayer, and inspired song are vital elements in growing in worship. Some of the richest worship in our community is initiated by spontaneous inspired prayer or song, or by prophecy.

5. *Following in the Spirit*. The prayer meeting leader should also help people learn to be sensitive to the way the Spirit is building praise. For example, it is important that people learn not to be anxious during periods of silence, that they learn how to sing in the Spirit in a way that is harmonious with the rest of the group, and so on.

There are a number of difficulties that will arise if worship does not take place properly at our prayer meetings: we won't hear the word of the Lord clearly, nor be able to obey it; our prayer meetings will become dry and lifeless, and certainly not a vehicle for preaching the gospel in power; there will be no growth in the exercise of spiritual gifts. The importance of worship in our meetings is clear. It is therefore necessary to know something about hindrances to worship, and how to correct them.

The music group, whether it is large or small, should consider its work a service to the Lord and to the prayer group. There is nothing so difficult to work with as a music group that doesn't serve: one that is independent, that is concerned more about style, skill, or cleverness than about helping people to sing, one that does not take the service seriously, or that does not practice regularly to try to improve.

Groups often encounter times when praise doesn't build, or when it peaks too quickly. This is a matter of the group not being able to persevere and continue in praise for a significant period of time. What is needed here is, simply, practice in praise and worship. In many cases, it is helpful to spend some time during the meeting expanding the group's vocabulary of praise beyond a few common expressions such as, "Praise you, Jesus," and, "Alleluia."

A problem which leaders may have is the presence of many newcomers in a meeting—something which can intimidate a leader. The important point is that newcomers should be *involved* in the group's praise: you shouldn't try to praise around them.

To make it easier for newcomers to become involved in the meeting, the leader should give clear and direct guidance. It is also helpful to have a warm, welcoming group to greet newcomers before the meeting begins.

Often, feelings of self-condemnation, unworthiness, and guilt act as obstacles to praise. When we encounter such feelings, we need to remember that we have a *commitment* to praise the Lord; it's not something we do only when we happen to feel like it. In fact, the most effective weapon against feelings like guilt and self-condemnation is praise. When God's people praise him, the evil one and his lies are rendered helpless.

We are indeed privileged as Christians to know the Lord and to be able to meet together to worship him. Our prayer meetings are both a sign and a source of life to the world. Prayer meeting leaders have a responsibility to make the most of opportunities to worship the Lord. Let us exercise our leadership responsibly, and form our brothers and sisters into the kind of worshipers who can rend the heavens and call down the blessings of God on a darkened world.

CHAPTER FOUR

HOW TO FORM
A MUSIC GROUP

Jim Rolland

M USIC is a powerful tool which God uses to bring people closer to himself. We have all experienced this at prayer meetings, conferences, and other Christian gatherings. Music can express worship and praise in ways that nothing else can.

Most prayer groups — especially smaller ones — need not worry about establishing a full-blown "music ministry." However, many groups will find it helpful to have a group of people take at least some responsibility for music.

The main purpose of a music group, obviously, is to minister God's love, God's word, and God's Spirit to his people. Too often, music is seen as merely a task to be performed. But if this is our attitude, God can't use it as effectively as he wants to. Music is a ministry in the truest sense of the word. It can evangelize, teach, inspire, encourage. It is a vital part of our worship, and should receive careful attention.

Surprisingly, the way to begin a music group is *not* simply to gather together a number of musical virtuosos. The group must be built on a firm foundation — the key to which is the establishment of loving relationships among the members. The effectiveness of a music group is determined more by the relationships within the group than by musical ability. The love of Jesus must be the very source of our music. We grow in this by spending time together, by praying, and playing together, and by honestly sharing our thoughts and feelings about our service. I'd rather have a music group made up of two people who really love each other than a group of twenty who don't.

Next, good leadership is a necessity if a music group is to get off the ground. By "leader" or "head," I don't mean "dictator." One person alone cannot accurately sense the Spirit. Therefore, input from others is needed. It is essential that the head be open to suggestions from the members of the music group and the leaders of the prayer group. The head does *not* have to be the best musician or singer. The important qualities are the ability to:

—help everyone learn to love one another, so that their service will flow out of Christ's love.

—present clearly the Lord's vision for the group: its purposes and goals. "Where there is no vision the people get out of hand" (Prov. 29:18, *JB*).

—care for individual members and help them grow in their musical ability. The goal should be to help each person become a mature, contributing member.

—organize and conduct rehearsals, and make final decisions on what music to use. The songs he or she chooses will affect the way the prayer group grows in its response to God.

—raise everyone's expectations, challenge them, call them on to greater heights, help them maintain an enthusiasm about serving the Lord. The attitudes of the head are a big part of this. If he or she is excited about the service, others will be also.

The leaders of the prayer group should be responsible for how the music group is developing, and for how music is used at prayer meetings. The music head should seek the help of, and submit to decisions made by, the leaders of the prayer group. This helps us avoid being possessive of "our" ministry, of being stubborn or glory-seeking.

The reason for establishing these relationships among heads is to facilitate a natural flow of the Spirit in our prayer meetings. I've found it best to have one person in charge of the meeting and one person in charge of music. The music group submits to the music head's direction, and the music head submits to the prayer meeting leader's direction.

Rather than stifling the Spirit, this allows a meeting to flow more freely. I've seen music groups hold summit conferences, in the middle of a prayer meeting, to decide what song to sing; I've even seen them argue over the choice of songs. Our goal should be to support, rather than obstruct, the spirit of the meeting.

To become good at anything, we must work at it and invest time in it. I don't know anyone who learned an instrument without committing some time to practice. We must be faithful in practicing, or we quickly lose our ability (this holds true for singers as well as for instrumentalists). Even if we don't have a lot of time for individual practice, we can at least play as much as possible in group situations. Guitarists in our music group don't play their instruments just once a week at prayer meetings. They also play daily in their personal prayer times, at family prayers, and so on.

For some, it might be helpful to buy an instruction book; music stores have many good books graded from "beginner" to "advanced." For some, it will be a good idea to take lessons. We should at least find someone to listen to us occasionally and give suggestions for improvement.

Group rehearsal is just as important as individual practice. We can't grow together, spiritually or musically, as isolated individuals. Time together is essential. Our group had to experiment with different rehearsal times. Evenings didn't work because people were too tired. Saturday morning was too busy, so we settled on Saturday afternoon. Of course, we couldn't find a time that was ideal for everyone, but we found the time that was best for most people.

We had to develop the attitude that rehearsals were important. We had to commit ourselves to be there and to put in our best effort. We can't learn to serve the prayer meeting with music if we come to rehearsals only sporadically, or if we don't put forth the effort to attend prayer meetings faithfully. We're called to develop not only our spiritual lives but also our musical ability: "Play with all your skill as you acclaim him!" (Ps. 33:3).

For small groups, with only a few people to choose from, integrating new people and instruments into the music group may not be a major concern. But it might be helpful to some larger groups if I share our experience of growth.

We started our music group four years ago. We didn't attempt to make ourselves into any particular kind of group; we didn't want our likes or dislikes to get in the way of what God wanted to do. We prayed that he would bring us the people and the instruments he wanted us to have.

At times, the group became unmanageable; things didn't seem to be flowing right. We then needed to take a realistic look at what the problem was. Sometimes we needed to "prune the branch" so that it could bear more fruit. This might mean trimming those people who couldn't come to rehearsals regularly, who were already over-committed, or who, on close examination, simply didn't have a gift to "minister" music. Many times this pruning was hard, but we saw the branch blossom and bear more fruit because of it. We must, of course, recognize that we are dealing with people who have feelings, and be sensitive to them. But we must also be faithful to the Lord and do that which really helps the whole group grow.

We've learned, somewhat to our surprise, that the question of what combinations of instruments are used is of secondary importance. If other things are working right, this area will take care of itself. We have radically changed our views of what is musically correct. We've found it important to give up preconceived ideas, and be more concerned with how effectively we're communicating the Lord's love.

"Commit your way to the Lord; trust in him, and he will act" (Ps. 37:5). The most important advice I can give to prayer groups starting up a music group is to step out and do it. Four years ago, we had no idea of how our group would grow and develop. But now we praise and thank God for what he has done with us.

We should all remember the story of the servant who buried his talent: the master sternly reprimanded him (Matt. 25:14-30). If we have musical talent, the Lord wants us to invest it in him so that it will be multiplied. Let us proclaim him through music, so that his name is glorified with an unending hymn of praise!

CHAPTER FIVE

TESTING PROPHECY

John Blattner

A FEW years ago I was part of a prayer group whose weekly meetings had developed a problem. One member of the group was in the habit of prophesying each week; the problem was that the person always said exactly the same thing, in precisely the same words, week after week, without variation. There was nothing wrong with the message itself — that God loved us and wanted us to spread his love — but because of its repetitiveness it began to disturb people.

Most members of the group gradually came to suspect that the message was, in some way, not truly from the Lord. But the leaders of the group, of which I was one, were afraid to confront the problem, and so the situation grew worse. Before long the prayer group began to experience doubts about the validity of prophecy. Even people who had themselves experienced a strong, consistent gift of prophecy became hesitant about exercising it.

The leaders finally decided that something had to be done. We spoke privately to the person and asked the person to stop prophesying at the meetings. (Surprisingly, the person agreed with us and even thanked us for our concern.) We also continued to encourage those with reliable prophetic gifts. Slowly, the group overcame its reticence about prophecy, and in time prophecy regained its proper place in the life of the group.

Many prayer groups experience confusion and uncertainty when it comes to prophecy. We can be so wary of doing anything that might "quench the Spirit" that we fail to test prophecy effectively. On the other hand, we can be overly strict, even harsh, in our judgments about others' prophetic gifts.

From the experience I've described above, I learned an important lesson about prophecy: it must be governed. It is the responsibility of the leaders of the group to test prophecy, to regulate the exercise of prophecy in the prayer meeting, and to help members of the group mature in their prophetic gifts.

Leaders often take a hands off approach when it comes to others' spiritual gifts, usually because of an understandable, but false, humility: "Who am I to pass judgment on a prophet?" But our concern to give our brothers and sisters the benefit of the doubt shouldn't be allowed to overshadow our responsibility to see that things go well in the group.

When a prophecy doesn't seem to sit right with people, it is the leaders who must give the group direction on how to respond to it. If a member of the group seems consistently to be off the mark in his or her exercise of the gift, the leaders must help that person overcome his or her weakness — or, in some instances, ask the person to stop prophesying for a while.

Corresponding to the leaders' responsibility to exercise authority over prophecy is the prophets' duty to submit to the leaders. I have sometimes heard prophets claim for themselves an authority apart from that of the leaders. Such an attitude is without justification. When Paul says that "the spirits of prophets are subject to prophets" (1 Cor. 14:32, RSV), he refers to a prophet's ability to decide whether or not to speak at a given time and in a given setting. This verse does not mean that a prophet is answerable only to himself regarding the validity of his message. Despite its spiritual nature, prophecy remains but one of many ministries within the body of Christ, all of which must operate under proper authority.

What are the specific responsibilities of leaders in helping prophecy to function well within their group?

Individual prophecies can and should be tested. The uppermost criterion is this: Is the message in keeping with Scripture, with Christian teaching? The principle is a simple one: The Holy Spirit does not contradict himself. We possess reliable guides to what God has revealed to men through his Spirit; we can trust that any message that is truly from the Holy Spirit will agree with previous revelation.

There is such a thing as false prophecy. By this I mean prophecy inspired by a spirit other than the Holy Spirit. Such prophecy is ordinarily not hard to recognize; its wrong content and harsh tone generally give it away.

In my experience, genuinely false prophecy is rare in the charismatic renewal. Far more common is what might be called "non-prophecy": a prophetic-sounding message whose source is neither the Holy Spirit nor an evil spirit, but the imagination of the person speaking.

The problem I described earlier was a case of non-prophecy. The message was clearly in line with Scriptural and church teaching, but was not directly inspired by the Spirit as a prophecy. The person involved simply had a very strong experience of a basic Christian truth and, being unfamiliar with the way prophecy works, felt led to share it in prophetic form.

But in order to prophesy, we need more than simply to have received a word from the Lord; we must also have been authorized by the Lord to speak it. Many times a person giving a non-prophecy is indeed in tune with the Spirit, and is correctly sensing something that the Lord is doing. But he or she has not been specifically commissioned to speak that word, and it thus lacks power.

An important caution must be made here. We should be careful not to brand as false a message that may be merely an instance of non-prophecy.

Another way to test a prophecy is through one of the other charisms — discernment of spirits. A person with this gift can often determine whether a prophetic message, or some portion of it, originates with the Holy Spirit, an evil spirit, or the speaker's imagination. A genuine gift of spiritual discernment is rare, though, and its validity is even more difficult to determine than that of prophecy. For this reason, it is generally unwise for a group to rely exclusively on one person's charism of discernment for testing prophecy. The pastoral judgment of the leaders (aided by such gifts of discernment as *are* available) is usually a more reliable barometer.

I have found that it is more important, and more effective in the long run, to test not individual prophecies but *prophets*. Put another way, the best guide to the validity of a prophecy is the life of the prophet himself. "For no good tree bears bad fruit, nor again does a bad tree bear good fruit; for each tree is known by its own fruit" (Luke 6:43-44).

In examining the life of a prophet, we might ask a number of questions. Has the person been a Christian long? Are they known to be mature and growing in the Christian life? Are they free of major sin? Does their daily life exhibit peace and order? Does their behavior give evidence of emotional or psychological instability? Unless these questions can be answered satisfactorily, it will be unwise to place confidence in a person's prophetic gift.

There is another question that could be asked: Is the person known well by the group? Unknown or itinerant prophets have caused great confusion in many groups. Their ministries should be tested with special rigor.

(Over a period of time, a solid, mature Christian can become recognized as a reliable prophet simply because his exercise of prophecy proves consistently fruitful and trustworthy. Such recognition can come only from careful discernment by the group, and especially the leaders, over several years.)

One further point about testing prophecy. It is not uncommon for groups to receive prophecies that direct them to take various concrete actions—often, actions that will have significant impact on the life of the group. Because of the difficulties involved in testing prophecies, we should be very cautious about obeying such messages unless we receive ample confirmation through several sources.

We may feel a desire to obey such prophecies immediately as a sign of faithfulness to the Lord. But if the Lord is trying to give us important direction, we can trust that he will honor our taking proper care in testing prophecy by confirming his word to us.

The leaders should take responsibility to see that prophecy functions smoothly in the prayer meeting. This includes knowing who should and should not prophesy. There may be some people in the group who, for various reasons, should not prophesy. We should tactfully ask them to refrain from prophesying.

Often it is important to exercise control over what is prophesied and when prophecies are given. Many prayer meetings become confusing and chaotic because people give weak, impure, or redundant prophecies, or because they stand up at random and prophesy. Many groups find that it helps ensure proper order to have people come forward to share their message with the leader of the meeting, or with an assistant assigned to the role, before speaking it. This way, important prophecies do not get lost in the crowd, weak prophecies and non-prophetic messages can be sifted out, and the flow of the meeting can be maintained. It is better to prevent a false or spurious prophecy from being given than to have to undo the confusion later.

The leaders of the group should encourage the development of prophecy among the group's members. We should be attuned to identifying those in our midst who seem to have a gift of prophecy. We should encourage those who prophesy well, and help them to prophesy better. It is often valuable to have all those in the group who prophesy meet together from time to time to pray together and support one another. We can also have people read books on prophecy. Bruce Yocum's *Prophecy* is an excellent practical guide for prophets as well as for leaders.

We should not let the potential problems inherent in prophecy discourage us. Thanks be to God for restoring this invaluable gift to us! "Would that all the people of the Lord were prophets! Would that the Lord might bestow his spirit on them all!" (Num. 11:29, *NAB*).

CHAPTER SIX

HOW TO GIVE
AN EFFECTIVE SHARING

Hal Langevin

S HARING at a prayer meeting, if it is done well, can be a very effective tool for drawing men and women closer to the Lord. Just as good teaching, music, and leadership are important for a good prayer meeting, sharing by members of the prayer group is also important. It can accomplish things that leading, teaching, or music cannot do.

In its simplest form sharing is telling others about something God has done in your life, in a way that will inspire them to love the Lord more deeply. Some examples of this would be telling of a personal experience of healing, an answer to prayer, a new revelation of God's love, overcoming a problem, a deeper understanding of God's word. Paul says it this way in his letter to Philemon: "I pray that the sharing of your faith may promote the knowledge of all the good that is ours in Christ" (Philem. 6, *RSV*).

The following are suggestions about how to share effectively at prayer meetings.

It's helpful to establish a goal before hand, that is, to determine what you are hoping to accomplish. We've found in our prayer meetings that when a person puts some thought into how to articulate what he has to say, God seems to use it more powerfully.

When you have a clear goal, it is easier to keep your remarks fresh and sharp, rather than dragging them out and trying to cover too much ground.

There can be many goals for a sharing. I would like to talk about three: evangelism, encouragement, and glorifying God. I recognize, of course, that these are not exclusive of one another. An evangelistic sharing, for example, does encourage others and glorify God. But these categories provide a helpful way to organize our thinking.

1. *Evangelism:* Sharing can be a tremendous way of bringing new people to a first commitment, or deeper commitment, to Jesus. An evangelistic sharing presents some aspect of a relationship with Jesus in a way that excites the listeners to want the same thing for themselves.

People tend to identify with others in situations similar to their own. Students can relate most easily to a fellow student telling how God worked in his life, while businessmen might best be evangelized by a personal story from a businessman who has overcome familiar pressures by the power of Jesus. In other words, the people who speak in prayer meetings will tend to attract similar kinds of people. Thus, we have found it works well to encourage sharings from a variety of age groups, occupations, and from both men and women.

A man recently told at one of our prayer meetings how God has restored his marriage over the last six years. It was a very moving description of how God had taken him and his wife from the state of separation, with major obstacles in their relationship, and brought them to a very stable, committed marriage and family life. That very night another man had come with his estranged wife to the prayer meeting for the first time. They had been separated for the past year. The wife was a Christian, and had been praying for her husband and for the restoration of their marriage. Upon hearing what the power of Jesus had done in the speaker's marriage, the husband made significant steps forward in his commitment to the Lord. As a result, his marriage has been restored and his whole family is now following the Lord.

We have seen God use sharings to bring many individuals to an initial commitment to Christ, as well as to a deeper commitment to the community.

2. *Encouraging Others.* Another goal of sharing is to encourage brothers and sisters. This might involve explaining how one has overcome a difficult circumstance by the grace of God, how God has answered prayer, how a problem in a personal relationship was worked out, or how grace has been at work in one's life in some other way.

Recently at one of our meetings a man told how he had been unable to make ends meet. He and his wife prayed that God would intervene and provide the funds to meet their financial commitments. In the following week, on three separate occasions, he received money from unexpected sources, which covered his needs. This report encouraged all of us to have greater faith in God. Encouraging one another is a major way of receiving grace and being called on more fully to the Christian walk.

3. *Glorifying God.* This is sharing that exalts the Lord for his marvelous actions. One of the best of this type that I've heard was given by a man telling of the miraculous healing of his daughter. His daughter had been hit by a truck while riding her bike. As the driver ran to help the girl, the truck slipped out of gear and ran over her a second time. She was seriously injured, with many broken bones, and lay unconscious in the hospital for several days.

The entire prayer group began interceding for the girl and her family. At the family's request, a priest came and anointed the girl for healing. The girl regained consciousness immediately. Scabs dropped from her abrasions, and her bones were instantly healed. As this was described, the entire prayer group broke into worship and praise and truly did experience the glory of God.

This is a very dramatic example of glorifying God. There are many other ways that God works sovereignly in our lives. These too can be shared to the glory of God.

How can we share in the most effective way? Here are some suggestions. Many of these are standard public-speaking techniques, and many I learned from hearing countless people speak at prayer meetings.

1. *Preparation.* In preparing to speak we need to ask Jesus what he wants us to bring to the meeting to help strengthen our brothers and sisters. Ask the Lord, "What should I share?"

— Know what you are going to say. A simple outline with a few major points is easy to prepare and extremely helpful.

— A Scripture passage can be a good starting or ending point. Using God's word founds one's remarks clearly on the Lord.

— Discuss what you are going to say with someone before you speak to the group. Feedback can sharpen and improve your sharing by showing you which points to highlight and which to delete.

— Plan a clear, concise ending and use it. Do not ramble. If you search for the perfect ending, you will never find it.

2. *Delivery.* Stand up and speak up. Although elementary and simple, this is essential. Remember both you and what you say are important. Speak with that conviction. If microphones are used, find out the proper way to use the microphone beforehand.

— Be positive. Avoid negative words about yourself, other people, and other organizations. Statements such as, "This prayer group really knows how to praise the Lord so much better than the one I used to belong to," praises one group at the expense of another.

— Avoid jargon. Speak so that both first-timers and long-standing members can understand you. Avoid such expressions as "saved," "God laid it on my heart," "The Lord told me," and "I've been convicted." These can turn people off and prevent them from understanding your message. Speak as you would at your job or in a classroom.

— Be straightforward and relaxed. If you are at ease, people listening will be, too. Avoid mannerisms like swaying side to side, jingling the change in your pockets, playing with the microphone cord. Avoid "ah-uh," "sort of," "you know," "really," and so on. These distract people and prevent them from fully responding to your sharing.

— Be practical. People can have a hard time relating to your "glorious, wonderful, transformed" life, even though it may be all those things. Be specific about what God has done for you — tell how he healed you, answered your prayer, met your financial need. Say something concrete and tangible that people can grasp.

— Focus on the Lord. It is better to hear about what the Lord is doing for you than what you are doing for the Lord.

— Don't be too personal. There are some things that should be shared only with a few trusted friends. These might involve personal sins, difficulties in personal relationships, certain temptations, and so on. The details of such things should not be shared at a public gathering.

— Share what happened to *you*. You lose credibility if you try to explain something very distant from your actual experience. Don't try to describe what has happened to your wife's third cousin's brother-in-law.

— Be attentive to your listeners. Make sure people can hear and understand you, that you have good eye contact. If you notice that people are losing interest, you may have been speaking too long. Try to conclude as soon as possible.

"There are different gifts but the same Spirit; there are different ministries but the same Lord; there are different works but the same God who accomplishes all of them in everyone. To each person the manifestation of the Spirit is given for the common good" (1 Cor. 12:4-8, *NAB*). The ability to relate one's experience of God to others is a gift of the Holy Spirit. We are in an age when all mankind needs to hear of the mighty works of our Lord. This responsibility falls not on a few Christians, but on all of us.

It is God's plan that his word be spoken. It must begin with us in our homes, prayer meetings, and churches. What begins as a simple sharing at a prayer meeting has a part in what God wants to accomplish. As we speak in our prayer meetings, we can expect the Lord to work powerfully.

II.

Identity, Leadership, and Unity

A strong prayer group knows who it is. Its members share a common understanding of what the Lord has called it to be. Its leaders translate that vision into concrete goals and actions, and help hold the group together when differences emerge.

CHAPTER SEVEN

CHECKLIST FOR RENEWAL

Gabe Meyer

Iɴ our day, God has raised up prayer groups in the charismatic renewal for the renewal of the church and the transformation of the world. As prophetic witnesses in parishes, congregations, and ecumenical groups, they are called to evangelization, reconciliation, healing, and service for the whole body of Christ.

How can our prayer groups actually become these effective instruments of renewal? How can we build our groups in a way that enables them to have maximum impact on the church and on society? I think there are three main goals we need to work toward: to foster the growth of strong prayer groups, to strengthen weak prayer groups and discourage their needless proliferation, and to see that prayer groups join forces as much as possible.

There are seven characteristics that I use to identify what I would call a strong prayer group.

1. *The quality of worship.* One of God's basic purposes in raising up prayer groups is to create people who know how to worship him.

By quality of worship, I mean such things as persevering in

praise, devoting a substantial portion of the meeting to prayer, making use of the many forms of worship that God has given us, seeing that music functions effectively in the prayer meeting, and so on.

2. *The exercise of spiritual gifts.* Does the group experience strong, stable, prophetic input? Are there people with a gift for exhortation, for calling other people on to respond to the Lord? Is the Lord raising up people who have a gift for preaching, for teaching? The degree to which these and other spiritual gifts are operating is an important indicator of the basic strength of a group.

3. *The strength of commitment.* How central is the prayer group in the lives of the people who belong to it? Is there a core of committed people within the group?

One way to measure commitment is to ask a hypothetical question of yourself: if you were offered a job next week that required that you be transferred to another city, would the prayer group figure in your decision whether to accept the job? This does not mean that you would automatically reject the job offer because of the prayer group, but would the group be an important consideration to you?

4. *The development of leaders.* Groups need not only people who can direct prayer meetings but leaders whom others will follow, who know how to follow the Lord themselves and can bring others into the fullness of Christian life.

5. *The accumulation of wisdom.* Wisdom, in the Bible, means practical knowledge gained from experience. When your group has a problem, how do you handle it? Do you ignore it, try to forget it? Do you simply assume the Lord is testing you, just grin and bear it? Or do you actively investigate the source of the problem, consider ways to resolve it, and try to implement a solution? Most important, do you remember what the Lord has taught you, so that you'll be able to deal with similar problems when they arise in the future?

6. *The pursuit of the Lord's vision.* We need to be concerned not with our own ideas of what the prayer group should be or do but with the Lord's desires. It is his plan and purpose, not

necessarily our own perspective or outlook, that we should pursue.

7. *Effective unity with other groups.* The key word is "effective." We need to find concrete ways of supporting one another in our service to the Lord.

Of course, none of our prayer groups completely meet all the criteria I have listed above. We all have room for improvement in one area or another.

But there are many prayer groups that experience weakness in a number of crucial areas. These are the groups that most need to examine who they are and what they are doing, and seek the Lord about how their service ought to continue.

A weak group, in the sense in which I am using the term, is a group that is doing well simply to exist, let alone have an impact on the surrounding society or be a source of life and strength for others. Such a group would lack a number of important things:

1. *It lacks sufficient understanding of Scripture and church life.* Prayer groups need people, especially leaders, who can help others understand how to relate to the church, how to avoid basic errors in Scripture interpretation, doctrine, and practice.

2. *It lacks the ability to provide basic Christian teaching.* It has no resources for instructing people in how to love one another, how to pray, how to be open to spiritual gifts, and so on.

3. *It lacks power in the exercise of spiritual gifts.* Often accompanying this is a lack of the means to discern the validity of such gifts as prophecy, teaching, and revelation.

4. *It lacks committed, stable leadership.* In many prayer groups, it is never quite clear who the leaders are, or the leaders are never fully accepted by the group. Repeatedly, leaders become frustrated and quit, and there is no effective way for the group to select new, competent leaders.

Any group can have problems in this area from time to time, but a weak group is one that experiences them often.

5. *It lacks a committed core group.* A prayer group needs to have a core of people who can be counted on to stick with it when the going gets rough. Groups that lack this core will find it impossible to handle difficulties well.

6. *It lacks the ability to handle disagreements.* Many prayer groups are so torn internally by factions and disputes that they actually become a source of division in their parish or congregation.

Notice that in listing the characteristics of strong and weak prayer groups, nothing has been said about the size of the group.

We all have a tendency to equate bigness with strength, and smallness with weakness. Thus, when we think of strengthening our group, we may automatically think of finding ways to make it larger.

But this line of reasoning is not entirely sound. True, a larger group will have access to more resources, and thus have a greater *potential* for strength. But size is not the primary determinant. Small groups can be quite strong, and large groups can be quite weak. We should not let ourselves think that because our group is small it cannot be an effective instrument of renewal — nor should we let our large size blind us to areas of weakness that might be present.

Groups that recognize themselves in my description of a "weak" prayer group need to ask themselves some hard questions. Do we have the gifts and wisdom we need to be an instrument of renewal? Is the Lord calling us to change, or even to disband?

I believe that many weak prayer groups, if they seek the Lord's will earnestly and honestly, will discover a need to make some fundamental changes in their conceptions of who they are and where they fit into the Lord's overall plan. In some cases it might even be best to discontinue a particular prayer group, and we should be open to the Lord pointing that out to us.

In many cases, however, what the Lord will want us to do is to join ourselves together with other, stronger, groups. There are a number of practical ways in which this can be done.

First, groups that have some weaknesses but that are basically sound can find other groups to serve as models and resources. Find a larger, stronger group that already looks like what the Lord is calling you to become. Ask that group to teach you, to pool resources with you. Ask its leaders to work with your leaders. Find out how they handled the problems you're now facing, and adapt their solutions to your situation.

For some groups, it will make more sense to simply combine with other groups, or to cluster around a stronger group. For example, several small, weak groups could combine to form a new, larger, stronger, area-wide group. Or a weak group could attach itself to a stronger group, continuing to meet by itself perhaps, but making the stronger group the main focus of its service and commitment.

Whatever configurations develop, prayer group leaders in an area should get together regularly, specifically as leaders, to pray together, to develop relationships as brothers and sisters in the Lord, and to seek the Lord's vision for their prayer groups in real humility.

Finally, we should expect the Lord to guide us as we try to serve him more effectively. I emphasize the word *expect*. We can be assured that God is at work in the charismatic renewal, and that he will provide wisdom and courage and strength to those who ask him. As we place our prayer groups more into his hands, we can trust him to reveal to us what we need to know to make our prayer groups into more effective tools for his work of renewal.

CHAPTER EIGHT

WHO ARE WE?

Bob Duggan

How can a prayer group discover its identity, its purpose? Lots of people in prayer groups, especially leaders, tug at the problem of "Who are we?" and "What are we trying to do?" The answers have to do with God's call and our response. They have to do with discerning God's vision for the group.

There are different kinds of prayer groups. Two ways of identifying a group are to look at its composition — who belongs and on what basis — and to look at its structure and objectives — how it is related to the church and to other groups, and what its objectives are.

Cardinal Leo Joseph Suenens describes several kinds of groups in his book, *Ecumenism and Charismatic Renewal: Theological and Pastoral Orientations.*

All-Catholic. The all-Catholic group will have Catholics as leaders and most of its participants will be Catholic, although others will be welcome. It is under the authority of the local pastor or bishop. Its teachings come from a Catholic background, and it celebrates the liturgical times and feasts of the year. The sacraments are important, and the eucharist, especially, is celebrated whenever possible. Other specifically Catholic areas

(Mary and the saints, for example) are freely opened.

Such groups should make their Catholic identity clear to participants when they are invited to attend meetings.

Ecumenical. Ecumenical prayer groups have joint participation by Catholics, Orthodox, Anglicans, and Protestants, or some mixture thereof. This kind of group has a concern for differences among Christians and somehow seeks to foster the reunion of the churches.

The ecumenical group may be sponsored by members of one Christian body and thus be Catholic-ecumenical or Lutheran-ecumenical, and so on. In such a case the leadership, as well as most of the members, will be from the sponsoring church body. If it is Catholic-ecumenical, it will serve mainly Catholic members but also will allow for Protestant and Orthodox expressions. Much depends on mutual agreement. For example, if a Catholic eucharist is celebrated, there will normally be other eucharistic services for those of the various church bodies.

In other ecumenical groups, the leadership comes from more than one church body. The membership is explicitly open to participants from various church bodies on an equal basis. The focus is on what all members have in common and on common goals. Normally such groups bring up matters on which members disagree only insofar as such discussions help advance the common goal.

Some ecumenical groups may have activities which focus on church unity. Here members represent various church bodies in perhaps a discussion of the differences among the churches. Such discussion is best done by people in leadership who are well-grounded in their own traditions and are aware that the task at hand demands great sensitivity.

Nondenominational. Nondenominational groups function on the basis of what is common to all the Christian traditions represented in the group. They usually do not focus on what church a member belongs to, nor do they discuss differences between churches. They avoid certain areas of doctrine.

In some cases this can stem from an attitude of religious indifferentism ("We're all the same and it doesn't matter what church we belong to"). Speaking as a Catholic, I must insist that religious indifferentism in a group can be destructive because it does matter who you are and who I am. It does matter whether we are part of different churches. I cannot be indifferent to you or your church. The question is: how do we love one another and worship together without compromising who we are?

It is, of course, possible to be nondenominational as a group without falling into an attitude of indifferentism. Often a nondenominational approach facilitates certain kinds of Christian service, such as evangelism.

Many prayer groups take on the characteristics of more than one kind. For example, a group may function as a nondenominational group, but then decide to have a Catholic eucharist. Or a group may be Catholic and yet not want anyone to talk about Mary. This kind of overlapping is confusing. The more consistent we are in our identity, the more clearly we can relate to one another in love. Then our expectations of one another will be realistic and capable of being fulfilled. When our identity is explicit and consistent and our expectations are clear, frustration is drastically diminished.

A prayer group's identity also stems from its structural relationships and its goals as a group.

Parish. A parish prayer group is in submission to the pastor, who has at least given his approval of the group. Hopefully he is actively involved in some kind of shared leadership and most of its members belong to the parish. Any outreach ministry usually is centered in the parish.

Parish Renewal. This group will have the same characteristics as the parish group but its purpose is renewal of the parish. Obviously the pastor must be deeply involved, and the group will be more at the very heart of the parish. The group may aim at merely supporting the renewal of the parish under the leadership of the pastor in a shared ministry.

Regional. A regional group draws people from a wide geographical area. Members come from a number of parishes; the leaders also belong to one or more parishes.

A regional group frequently results from the merging of two or more smaller groups. It is not concerned with a particular parish but encourages each person to be faithful to his home parish.

Emphasis is usually on evangelism and teaching. Here more of
the gifts are exercised because numbers are larger and talents are
pooled. Hopefully the leadership works in concert with local
pastors who give their support.

"Just a Prayer Group." Several people, maybe a dozen, gather
in a home to pray and share. They support one another and listen
to God's word together. Everything is informal. Leadership is
minimal. Ministries are usually not developed, and there are few,
if any, formal teachings. The group's composition may range
from all-Catholic to nondenominational, but because of its infor-
mality there is less need for naming it. However, it is still important that expectations be clarified and made explicit.

A prayer group can be described both in terms of its composition and in terms of its structural relationships and goals. For
example, it could be an all-Catholic, parish renewal group, or a
regional, nondenominational group, or a Lutheran-ecumenical,
living-room group. Do not pick the label first and then try to fit it.
See who you are and then identify yourself to others.

Being able to answer the question, who are we? is a matter of
self-discovery. Sometimes the road to self-discovery is difficult,
but it is worth the struggle.

What we are talking about is the Lord's vision for the group. It
seems good to give a further description of the word "vision," so
that you know how I am using it. To have a vision is to grasp an
object with your eyes, mind, heart, or imagination. It is a
call from the Lord for a particular way of life or ministry. It is a
way to live the gospel. It is a direction in which to go. Frequently
the particulars of the vision are not given; it starts as a seed and
grows. A vision for a group gives it its main direction. From this
flow commitments and ministries.

This vision has to come from the Lord, through the group.
Someone may articulate it for the group, but the group must
accept it as a description of themselves. No one can impose it. As a
group shares and prays together, they slowly begin to grasp
something of what the Lord might be calling them to.

Ask yourselves some practical questions such as: why did you
come to this group? and, why do you stay? Have each member in
the prayer group talk for about sixty seconds and see what

emerges. It is not unusual that the same thing is repeated over and over and common themes emerge.

Some groups find it helpful to have an outsider sit in on these sharings. Invite one or two people with wisdom and the experience of hearing the Lord in groups. An objective person can be of immense value in restating what the group is saying.

It's important to perform what I call an "examination of consciousness." An examination of consciousness is different from what many of us know as the examination of conscience, a Catholic preparation for confession. The examination of consciousness is different because it stresses being conscious of how God has worked and is working in our lives. In prayer, we recall (remember to remember) how God has acted in our life and how we have responded to him. We detect the pattern of God's activity.

A group can do this rather easily. Recall how God has acted among you from the beginning until now. The more you do it, the easier it gets. What are the patterns of God's activity among the group? What is the Lord doing now? What has been our response?

A healthy prayer group knows who they are. They are wise to recount their history. It is their group's salvation history. It is important to recall and retell. "Remember how we used to gather in George's basement to pray? Then we moved to the social hall. Remember the fun we had together after the meetings?"

Examination of consciousness leads to the development of goals. When we share together we talk about what we want, what is in our hearts. The expression of desires leads to the formulation of goals. Goals state our intention. They say what we want to accomplish together.

When we choose goals we necessarily say yes to some and no to others. We cannot be both an all-Catholic and a nondenominational group at the same time. Setting priorities is important at this point. That means seriously looking at what is most important and choosing it.

There are many questions to ask. Questions can be a very helpful means of self-discovery, especially when this process is

approached in a prayerful, trusting environment. It might be a
simple question such as: why does everyone in the group come?
Ask each one and see what the answers are.

You may find that some in the group have a totally different
purpose from you for being at the prayer meeting. Some may
come just to praise and thank God. Others may come because
they believe this prayer group will renew the parish. If that is the
case, sooner or later the expectations of each will clash. If I expect
us to work at renewing the parish and you are perfectly content to
praise God and go home, then I am going to be frustrated and you
are going to be surprised. Thus clarifying expectations is a freeing
thing for the whole group.

Fear is a big obstacle. Many people are afraid to share their
feelings and desires. They can share something that happened on
the way to work, but they cannot freely open their hearts to
brothers and sisters.

Charismatics are sometimes afraid of thinking. Once we are
baptized in the Spirit, we frequently fall into a mindset which
says that if the Spirit is working, he will *tell* us and we do not
have to go through all this work. However, the Spirit often tells us
through our brothers and sisters, when we sit down and use our
minds as well as our other gifts for his kingdom.

Some people fear having outsiders come in to share and
observe, that is, people to help them discover their identity. It is
the old "dirty laundry" syndrome. If we wait until our act is
together before we get outside help, then we either will not need
help because we have it perfectly together (highly unlikely), or
we will not need help because we have withered up and blown
away.

Another problem is the failure to acknowledge the need to
identify ourselves and develop goals. It is important for the whole
group to know itself and work toward goals. You can hear the
Lord in one another and in yourselves. Trust him to work in this
way.

Jesus Christ is Lord. He is Lord of your prayer group. Let him
free you to be fully open with one another. The arm and leg are
different members but they have the same life-blood flowing

through them. What is the life-blood flowing through your group? What ever type it is, it is precious, especially when you pour it out for one another.

CHAPTER NINE

WHO SHOULD LEAD?

An Interview with Jack Brombach

Jack Brombach is a coordinator of the Servants of the Lord, a Christian community in Minneapolis, Minnesota.

Q: Leadership styles vary from prayer group to prayer group. In some, one person is responsible for leading; in others, several people share an informal, unstructured responsibility; and in others, pastoral teams lead the group. What type of leadership best supports a prayer group?

A: I don't think any one man or woman has all the gifts necessary to effectively lead a prayer group. A prayer group needs prophets, teachers, pastors, and people with a host of other gifts. A well-chosen, well-defined team of people can combine the gifts of various individuals and put them at the service of the group.

A team approach also protects the prayer group from the dangers inherent in leadership provided solely by one person. Members of a team submit their ideas to one another for testing and approval. The group can be sure that it isn't left to the untested discernment of one person.

Q: What qualities should a prayer group look for in a leader?

A: The guidelines that Scripture gives regarding the character of a bishop or an elder can be applied to leaders of prayer groups. The apostle Paul tells us that a bishop "must not be arrogant or quick-tempered or a drunkard or violent or greedy for gain, but hospitable, a lover of goodness, master of himself, upright, holy, and self-controlled" (Titus 1:7-8, RSV). He also insists that a person's family relationships should be working well (1 Tim. 3:4-5).

A leader should be loyal to the group, committed to what God wants to do there. He or she ought to be faithful in little things as well as in more important matters.

Further, an effective leader must be mature and emotionally stable. Does he conduct himself properly in his day-to-day life, in the prayer group, and in prayer meetings? Is his life characterized by an attitude of service, or is he eager to be the center of attention? Is he withdrawn, afraid of responsibility? Does he prophesy or share in response to his own need, or is he actually speaking God's word?

The Lord's warning about the dangers of building on sand (Matt. 7:24-27) can be applied to the leadership we establish in our prayer group. A group built on ineffective, immature leadership is not going to stand firm.

Q: How do a person's natural talents fit in?

A: The first consideration in choosing leaders should be whether or not their lives conform to the standards for leaders established in the Bible. But that's not the only test. A prayer group should also look for people who have a vision for what God is doing in the world today, who have good insight into Scripture, who exercise or are open to exercising the charismatic gifts. Further, leaders should have the ability to move people, to inspire them to respond to God's word.

Although a person's natural talents might strengthen his or her service as a leader, a prayer group should be careful not to fill key positions simply on the basis of natural gifts. Many groups will ask someone to teach at prayer meetings simply because he or she is a good school teacher. Or they'll find someone with a powerful voice and a degree of poise, and ask him or her to lead the prayer meeting every week. That's a dangerous way of establishing leadership for a prayer group.

Q: *Should priests, ministers, and nuns be selected as leaders?*

A: I think people tend to put clergy and members of religious orders in pastoral positions within the prayer group simply because of their position in the church. Now, I certainly don't think that the fact that a man is a priest should keep him from being on a pastoral team, but I don't think he should be placed on the team simply because he is a priest. The criteria for selecting pastoral leaders should apply to clergy and members of religious orders just as they apply to any man or woman.

Q: *You've touched on the topic of women serving as leaders. How do you feel about this?*

A: I think it's fine for a woman to be on the pastoral team of a prayer group as long as it intends to remain a prayer group. If it intends to move toward becoming a covenant community, then I think that serious consideration should be given to scriptural principles concerning the need for male leadership. However, I don't see any problem with men and women serving together on a pastoral team for a prayer group.

Here again, the biblical criteria should prevail: a woman's suitability as a leader should be determined by her maturity, stability, gifts, and so on. Women should neither be included nor excluded from pastoral teams simply because they are women.

Q: *Suppose a prayer group has been going along for a while under the leadership of an individual or an informal group of people. How do they go about establishing a clearly defined leaders team?*

A: The first thing they should do is fast and pray for the task they're about to undertake. Then they should agree that they're not going to race through the process. They ought to set aside a period of time—maybe a couple of months—in which to go through the various steps toward establishing leaders. They might even want to set a time limit or draw up a schedule for when they'll accomplish various steps in the process. From time to time they might want to bring in a recognized leader from the area who can advise them.

In his book, *Build with the Lord*, Bert Ghezzi suggests a good process. First, the group should spend some time discussing who they are as a prayer group. If they're a small group that meets every week, that's fine; they shouldn't necessarily see themselves as a small group destined to become a covenant community. They should realistically appraise what they are and work with that.

Next, they should consider what they need in terms of leadership. At this point, I'd recommend that everyone read some material on prayer group leadership and what a leader ought to be like. Discussion should accompany the reading. By the time this stage is complete, everyone should have a clear idea of the group's leadership needs.

After that, everyone in the group can write down the names of five or so people who would be good leaders. Then someone puts those names together and identifies a small group of people recommended by a significant portion of the group.

Q: Once a prayer group has identified a group of leaders, how do they ratify their decision to accept the leadership of the team?

A: The prayer group should make a public indication of their loyalty to the leadership they have chosen. For example, at a prayer meeting, they could all state aloud that they accept and will support the team. Then everyone could pray over the new leaders.

It's also helpful for the prayer group to put the responsibilities of the team in writing. This written statement doesn't have to be anything more than a good set of notes, but it should clearly indicate the kinds of authority the team will exercise and the support the group is expected to give the leaders. This certainly would not be a covenant agreement; it would simply be a statement that people could refer to later if things start to get a little fuzzy.

Q: Should members of a pastoral team serve indefinitely, or for some fixed period?

A: It's important that there be stability on the leaders team. It takes time for a group of people to establish the relationships needed to serve together effectively; this can't happen if there's rapid turnover. Leadership in the prayer group ought to be viewed as a long-range service.

This doesn't mean, "Once a leader, always a leader." For one thing, prayer groups can decide that new leaders will first serve on a trial or temporary basis—say, six months or so. After this time is up, the group can decide whether the person ought to continue as a leader. I don't mean that during this time the leader's every move is scrutinized. It is simply a time to honestly evaluate whether leadership is the right role for a given individual.

In a similar vein, it may become clear to a particular leader, and to the pastoral team as a whole, that his gifts lie in a different area. In such a case, it would certainly be appropriate for that leader to move to a different service. Christian leadership is not a position of status or a political appointment; it is a service. And as with any service, moving into or out of it shouldn't be an occasion for either pride or disgrace.

CHAPTER TEN

WHO CAN
WE HELP?

Gabe Meyer

I N our society there are many people who have no roots, no place where their problems can be dealt with. The supports that family and community would have provided them at one time are often lacking today. In fact, the anonymity of our society intensifies their difficulties.

To people with emotional problems, charismatic prayer groups provide a warm, loving atmosphere where, they may think, all their needs can be met. Consequently, prayer groups attract many people with emotional problems, and even a few with serious psychological illnesses.

In some ways this is a good thing. These people can be brought to the Lord, and can begin to experience his saving and healing power.

But difficulties arise. Such people frequently expect a prayer group to provide a lot of assistance or emotional security. Sometimes people with emotional problems are insistent about receiving help; they may gain a lot of attention and become the focus of the group's ministry. If a group does not really have the resources to provide this kind of help, its energies will be drained; services the group *is* capable of will be left undone, and the people with serious problems will not benefit very much.

Often people with major emotional or psychological problems will dominate the prayer group's meetings. Unless the leaders take action to prevent this, a bad spiritual tone is set when the group gathers to pray. This holds back the development of the group and alienates newcomers.

In a few instances, people with serious problems may even become harder to reach. Being baptized in the Spirit may give them a conviction that their abnormal behavior is in obedience to special leadings from the Spirit. Their problems become "canonized" and untouchable.

I would make six recommendations to leaders of charismatic prayer groups.

1. *Focus attention on building up the whole group, not on dealing with any particular problem.* The leaders of the group need to ask themselves, "What is the purpose of this prayer group?" For most prayer groups, the answer will be that the purpose is to provide opporunities for worship, evangelism, teaching, and the growth of loving, supportive personal relationships.

Leaders have a responsibility to see that these things happen. They should not neglect these responsibilities in order to help one or more individuals with serious problems. In most prayer groups, leaders will find that the pursuit of the prayer group's basic goals will demand all the time and energy they have available.

2. *Learn to recognize people who have serious psychological problems.* The sooner the leaders realize that someone has serious problems, the sooner they can decide what to do for that person and for the good of the prayer group.

One woman who was part of our group, for example, showed some possible indications of serious problems. She had steep emotional ups and downs, periods of elation and generosity — "I want to give my whole life to God" — alternated with times of depression and anger. This emotional instability created problems in the ways she related to other people — resentment, complaints of being unloved, difficulty holding jobs.

She was not fulfilling her responsibilities to her family. This is a critical sign for prayer group leaders to notice. Some people talk about doing great things for God, but are really trying to avoid dealing with problems at home and problems within themselves.

Another possible sign of serious emotional difficulty is love of controversy. In some people this is merely a wrong habit they need to change; but sometimes it indicates a deeper emotional problem.

Also, prayer group leaders should be quick to spot people whose thinking and behavior seem strange. People in the charismatic renewal sometimes have a weakness here; at first, something strange may seem to us to be rather spiritual. We should remember that when the Lord calls us into life in the Spirit, he doesn't call us to become strange.

3. *Be realistic about the prayer group's resources.* Leaders should not automatically assume that their group can help each person who comes to it. Almost always, more than an initial experience of God's power is required to heal deep-seated emotional difficulties. Healing requires the help of people who have wisdom and time available.

Usually, a prayer group cannot be the solution to serious psychological problems because the prayer group directly affects the person for only a couple of hours each week. But the environment, which may cause half the problem, has the person the rest of the week. Ultimately, many people can be helped only when they are brought out of their old environments.

Members of prayer groups, particularly newer members, may want to help people with serious problems, but often do not recognize that they are not equipped to do so. When we see someone who is very needy, it is hard to accept our limitations. We need to understand that it is not we who save, nor the prayer group that saves: only Jesus saves. We may be a part of the process. But most prayer groups can be only a limited part of the healing process for a very troubled person. Perhaps the process will have to be completed in a more total environment; perhaps the person should be referred to a professional counselor.

4. *Undertake to help people with serious problems only on the basis of clear agreements.*

Most prayer groups are simply not in a position to attempt such an undertaking. This recommendation applies to the rare groups which can.

First of all, the leaders need to agree among themselves about what the person needs and what the prayer group can do to help. They need to define their goals and approach.

Second, the leaders need to tell the person what problems they see, and ask the person if he or she is willing to accept help. If not, nothing can be done.

5. *Do not put emotionally or psychologically troubled people in positions of responsibility.* Leaders sometimes do this to give such people a sense of self-worth or acceptance, but the people cannot cope with the responsibility. The people with serious problems are not helped, and neither are those they are supposed to serve.

6. *Leaders must protect the prayer meetings from disturbances.* The prayer meeting leader has a responsibility to correct problems caused by disruptive behavior or misguided exercise of spiritual gifts.

The leader's first responsibility is to the whole body, to see that it is directed properly. Second comes his concern to see that an individual who has caused a problem is dealt with compassionately.

If a person with serious problems acts in a disruptive way during a prayer meeting, the leader should deal with the situation in a direct, straightforward way. Someone else in the group can take the person to another room; in a large prayer group, a regular group of ushers can do this. The person should be cared for, but outside rather than within the meeting.

When problems at meetings are caused not by a newcomer but by someone who attends occasionally or regularly, the leaders should talk to the person about his or her participation in the group. It might be appropriate to tell the person not to speak out at the meetings or not to do other things which do not build up the other members of the group.

The Lord can accomplish a great deal of good through the prayer groups in the charismatic renewal. The more we build carefully and wisely, the more effective instruments our prayer groups will be for his work in the world.

CHAPTER ELEVEN

EVALUATING OUR SERVICE

John Evans

IT's easy to understand why evaluation is an unpopular subject. Our competitive society subjects us to all kinds of criticism. It begins when we go to school and continues for most of our lives. The word evaluation may bring to mind unpleasant or even traumatic experiences, which undermined our self-confidence and, in some instances, left painful wounds.

Most of us see our prayer groups as havens from the competition and rejection that characterize our world — and rightly so. We want to find acceptance, not more rejection; consequently, we recoil at the suggestion that our work for the Lord and his people ought to be regularly evaluated.

But good order and effective service are impossible without assigned responsibilities and periodic evaluation. People who serve in their prayer groups on pastoral teams, Life in the Spirit Seminars, or other groups, should make regular evaluation sessions a part of their service.

Fortunately, Christians can learn to evaluate one another's service without drawing blood. In fact, evaluation can be liberating and upbuilding when undertaken in Christian love and commitment. When we realize that we're not going to be rejected for making a mistake, we're more inclined to trust one another and to believe that the Lord can actually help us through evaluation sessions. "Be open with the wise, he grows wiser still; teach a virtuous man, he will learn yet more" (Prov. 9:9, JB).

Paul's definition of love in 1 Corinthians 13 is an ideal summary of the virtues that should characterize every evaluation session. We should be kind, humble, and courteous from start to finish, and quick to acknowledge and commend all that has been done well. We should never allow ourselves to take offense or become resentful. We ought to rejoice as we discover the Lord's truth — even when his view of the situation differs from ours — but not make our brothers and sisters feel defeated or humiliated. Comments such as, "*Now* you're in the Lord," or "See, this is what we've been telling you all along," can turn good fruit rotten on the spot.

Rather, we should encourage people to try again, to rely more on help from the prayer group next time, and to expect a better outcome. This encouragement is one of the primary purposes of evaluation. Criticism without support produces frustration, anxiety, a replay of the original problem, and new difficulties (usually a crisis of confidence and damaged relationships).

Leaders should lay the groundwork day by day for loving evaluation; if they are habitually compassionate, perceptive, and tactful, their brothers and sisters will have no reason to fear their evaluation. They will see it as an opportunity to recognize and foster one another's gifts, to consider new assignments for the good of the body, to go deeper into the life of the Lord.

Evaluations are more successful if they occur regularly than if they occur sporadically. People learn to take them in stride: no one is inhibited by anxiety, so discussion moves freely; when there is disagreement, it is congenial and creative. Sessions should be scheduled frequently, perhaps every few months; a long interval means a long agenda. When the agenda gets too long, establishing priorities becomes a vexing matter; some problems don't get sufficient attention and reappear, bigger and more ominous than ever, on the next agenda. Worst of all, groups that don't conduct regular evaluations become crisis-oriented. Because they lack the means to discover difficulties early, all their problems are big ones.

The prayer group leaders should assume responsibility for seeing that evaluation sessions occur regularly and rightly, but they should not try to do everything themselves. Heads of service groups should be consulted, and any member of the group who has suggestions ought to be heard.

Before the evaluation, those who are to conduct it should formulate comments and questions as specifically as possible. Instead of asking, "How do you feel the Life in the Spirit Seminar teachings went this time?" they should ask, "How many people attended the sign-up session? How many of these people were baptized in the Holy Spirit? Were discussion leaders able to handle questions directed to them?" A copy of the agenda should be put in the hands of everyone involved in an evaluation several days ahead, so that they can prepare adequately.

In planning an evaluation session, some kind of standard should be formulated to measure performance. These standards should be realistic. When evaluating Life in the Spirit Seminar teams, for example, we shouldn't expect presentations on a par with talks at the last regional conference. Being realistic doesn't mean being complacent or satisfied with things that are clearly not going well. We should always strive for the best, but remember that we are dealing with imperfect people and limited resources.

Anything we do together should begin with prayer. At evaluation sessions, the group should pray for unity of heart and mutual trust, for the Lord's guidance, for protection against anger and resentment, for new life.

At the outset, one of the leaders should explain what the objectives are and how the evaluation will proceed. This is the time to be reassuring. It is best to begin by commending people for what they have done well. Often, an entire evaluation will consist of exchanging ideas for improving what is basically a good situation.

Sometimes, though, we need to point out problems. In doing so, we should be specific, concise, and objective. We should avoid hinting, or beating around the bush, in the hope that people will get the point without our having to make it. Evasion is not kindness; it is devious and manipulative behavior. Equally objectionable are sarcasm, unkind jokes, and invidious comparisons ("Carolyn and Grace don't seem to be having any trouble with their discussion groups, Agnes. What's wrong with you?").

At no point during the session should anyone ignore a problem, or fear candor and honesty. Leaders should not be so worried about the effects of their criticism that they fail to point out weaknesses. Some of us find it difficult to criticize people who are trying hard. In the name of love we avoid making constructive criticism, even though we know that real love seeks what is best for others, correcting them if necessary (Heb. 12:5-9).

Ideally, we should learn to admit our mistakes, resist dejection, and welcome the help that we need to "live the kind of life that God wants" (1 John 3:22). But the just man falls seven times a day, and an evaluation is, for many, a big stumbling block. We should expect that sometimes people will be somewhat self-protective, and not reprove them too hastily.

When someone reacts emotionally, it is unproductive to insist, "You shouldn't feel that way," and immediately preach a sermon about self-control. The situation calls for understanding and reassurance, not reproach. "Steve, your anger tells me this matter is very important to you. Because I love and respect you, I'd like to urge you to be open and frank. Don't be afraid that I'll be judgmental or unable to see your point of view. Tell me again how you see it, and then let's look at your reasons for viewing it that way." This does not encourage emotional self-indulgence. Rather, it redeems a troublesome situation and creates a solid foundation for constructive discussion about emotions at another time.

We can expect the Lord to enable us to relate patiently and gracefully with our brothers and sisters. The Lord will give us vision and balance so that we can resist the temptation to retaliate if stung by an unjust or intemperate remark. We can also restrain ourselves from going beyond the agenda into people's personalities. "All right, Ed, you've spent twenty minutes complaining about this evaluation, now let's talk about your real problem. It's you. Your attitude isn't right. You've got to learn how to respond to criticism." Now Ed may well need correction and counselling, but not during a meeting that was convened for another purpose. Much better to say simply, "Ed, let's stick to the agenda. If you're having problems with our leadership, we should discuss that later."

Evaluation can be a vital part of our service to the Lord. Problems, like sins, weaken when they are brought into the light, and mature, trustworthy Christians can lead us deeper into the Lord's truth, to a depth where the world and our weaknesses cannot easily follow. We should regard evaluation as a source of divine light, helping us to "go on growing in the grace and in the knowledge of our Lord and Savior Jesus Christ" (2 Pet. 3:18).

CHAPTER TWELVE

A CHANGE OF HEART OR A CHANGE OF LEADERS?

Kevin Perrotta

WHO should lead the prayer group? The question has received a lot of attention in recent years at conferences, in books and magazine articles, and, of course, in prayer groups. Much has been said about the gifts and personal qualities the leaders of the prayer group should have.

The side of the selection process that has gotten the most attention is how to get the right people into leadership. The side that has received the least attention is what to do when it seems that one or more of the group's present leaders are unqualified for their responsibility.

That's the more difficult side. We feel more comfortable telling someone that they have a gift than that they don't—and how much easier it can be to hear it!

But while the leaders of a prayer group may find it hard to deal with a situation in which it seems that not all of them belong in the leaders' group, eventually they will need to face up to the problem and solve it. The question of leadership is crucial for a prayer group; without the right leadership, the group will not grow as the Lord intends.

What can prayer group leaders do to see that people who are unqualified step out of leadership? No single solution exists, because prayer groups vary greatly from each other. But here are some suggestions that will help in most cases.

1. *Identify the problem.* Problems with leadership do not necessarily mean that someone should leave the leaders' team. The difficulties might point to other weaknesses.

Sometimes problems stem from confusion about the group's goals. Are we supposed to work for parish renewal or not? Should the prayer group be strongly characterized by our predominant church background — Catholic, Lutheran, Presbyterian — or should we strive to be a gathering of all kinds of Christians? Is our goal to remain a prayer group or to move toward deeper commitments to one another?

Without a common vision that everyone explicitly agrees on, the leaders of the prayer group may find themselves working at cross purposes. If there is no overall agreement about what kind of prayer group we are, it may seem that someone is failing as a leader when actually the person needs some clarification about what he or she is supposed to be doing.

Sometimes the difficulties arise from a lack of good personal relationships among the leaders. When leaders don't know one another well enough, friction and misunderstandings may develop. A leader may be experiencing difficulties because he or she is not receiving support and encouragement in developing as a leader.

Fr. Bob Duggan, head of a service team for Catholic prayer groups in the archdiocese of Detroit, has helped numerous groups examine these questions. "We help them ask themselves: What is the Lord's call to this group? What responsibility should the leaders have for implementing it? What authority? Do the leaders have the gifts and time to do what they're supposed to do? Are the leaders growing in a solid relationship with each other?"

Sometimes the prayer group needs a change of heart rather than a change of leaders. Members' objections to certain leaders may stem from resentment, jealousy, or an unwillingness to accept even a moderate degree of authority.

An editor of a Christian magazine that publishes advice for prayer groups told me he occasionally gets letters complaining about prayer group leaders. "Often it seems pretty clear to me that the leaders aren't doing anything very wrong. I sometimes write back and tell people I think they ought to give their leaders more support."

Finally, the problems with leadership may indicate that one or some of the leaders are not suited to the task. It may be that a person does not have a gift for leading prayer meetings, teaching people practical things about the Christian life, or organizing activities. He or she may work hard, support the prayer group, and be a faithful servant, but simply not have leadership abilities.

Or the person may have personal problems: hostility when offered advice or evaluation, consistent failure to carry out agreements and fulfill responsibilities, unwillingness to work as a member of a team, emotional instability, serious family problems.

2. *It's usually best to be direct.* By this I don't mean that we should seek confrontations but that we should avoid roundabout methods.

For example, most of the leaders of the prayer group might think that someone should no longer be a leader, but out of fear of hurting the person's feelings — or fear of how the person might react — they don't tell him. Instead, they invent something else for him to do, like leading a "growth group" on the same night the leaders' team meets. "Obviously," they point out, "you'll have to withdraw from the leaders' group."

Or they might begin hinting that he would be more suited for something else; or they might stop encouraging him at all.

Indirect methods often produce resentment. As Gabe Meyer, a leader of the City of Angels community in Los Angeles, has said, "People are usually smart enough to figure out what's going on, and while they may not say anything, underneath they feel bitter."

Normally the better way is to go to the person and talk about whether it's right for him or her to be a leader. This approach requires candor, sensitivity, and loyalty.

Often such honest sharing of views will expose the fact that the person would like to step out of leadership. Many prayer group leaders find themselves overburdened, either because they don't have enough time or don't think they have the gifts to lead the group. (Of course, some leaders who feel this way simply need help getting their schedules in order or delegating their work, or need some encouragement.)

3. *Get outside help.* In many prayer groups there isn't anyone who is recognized as the overall head of the leaders' team and who has the wisdom and skill to deal with disagreement about whether someone should leave the leaders' team. "In most groups the leadership is not strong enough to work smoothly through the difficulties and feelings of rejection that can come up," Gabe Meyer has said.

In the absence of such leadership, the group's leaders would do well to seek help from a strong nearby prayer group or community or from some regional group such as a diocesan service committee for the charismatic renewal.

4. *Sometimes, consult the prayer group.* Answering questions about the direction of the prayer group and the kind of leadership it needs may involve consulting the whole prayer group; that is, all the regular members.

This step should be taken carefully. As one leader of a large prayer group commented, "Even in well-functioning groups some people will feel the wrong people are leading the group. You want to get some input from the group without stirring up the people who are always dissatisfied."

5. *Establish a process for choosing and evaluating leaders.* In some prayer groups, there is no crisis in leadership, but the group would benefit from a change. Setting up a leader selection process may solve this problem.

Joe Breault, leader of the Community of God's Love, in Rutherford, New Jersey, describes how this happened in one large prayer group.

"Things were going okay, but the leaders felt the Lord was saying they needed a review procedure for the leaders. They didn't adopt a democratic plan and vote on the leaders. Instead they explained to everyone what kind of people should be leaders, and they had a day of prayer and fasting. Then they asked everyone to name who they thought should be leaders.

"All the current leaders were supported except one—who was the founder of the group. The other leaders talked to the person and suggested it was time to step out of leadership, so the person resigned."

Leading a group through a one-time consultation to solve a particular leadership problem can raise a lot of touchy, personal items. Many leaders of prayer groups don't have the skills to do it. But establishing a *regular* procedure for choosing and evaluating the leaders can take some of the personal pressure off the situation.

These five suggestions concern how to handle current problems. There are also several preventive measures prayer group leaders can take:

— When leaders are chosen, let there be a clear agreement they will serve for a certain period—a year, say—and will be evaluated. If it then seems a person should no longer be on the leaders' team, the transition represents the results of an experiment, not a personal failure. (During the year, the person shouldn't be subjected to unremitting scrutiny by everyone in the group.)

— Leaders should work at developing good personal relationships with one another.

"Leaders ought to be able to talk with one another about their gifts and abilities," Gabe Meyer said. That means they need to know, trust, and care for each other. Then if it seems that someone should leave the team, the question can be discussed peacefully, without feelings of rejection.

Also, with mutual support, the leaders of the prayer group can help each other learn how to guide the group.

— Teach the whole group that leadership is a kind of service not a source of status (Mark 10:42-45). This will help leaders to accept evaluation (because they want to serve as well as possible) and to leave the team if that seems right (because they want to serve where they are best suited).

As the group takes on this Christian perspective on leadership, they will also be better able to pick the right leaders. There will be a stronger tendency to choose people who have the right gifts to serve as leaders, rather than to make people leaders as a reward for their hard work.

—Discourage one-person rule. It is much easier to have one person leave the leaders' team than to have the group's only leader step aside. And a team works better than one person to lead a prayer group.

CHAPTER THIRTEEN

DISAGREEMENT WITHOUT DIVISION

John Blattner

IN most prayer groups things go well most of the time. The leaders lead and the group responds; the weekly prayer meeting is a source of inspiration and support; members grow in love for one another as brothers and sisters in Christ. Minor difficulties pop up from time to time but generally are resolved satisfactorily.

Sometimes, however, significant problems arise. What at first looked like a relatively small disagreement suddenly escalates into a major controversy. Relationships are strained, even broken. Factions begin to form around divergent points of view. The leaders find themselves bewildered and embattled. Almost before anyone realizes what is happening, the prayer group is paralyzed. Ultimately the problem is "resolved" by the group splitting in two or disintegrating entirely.

This scenario is all too familiar. Most of us know of — and some of us belong to — a group that has had such an experience. It doesn't have to be this way. Fractious disagreement and divisiveness find no place in God's plan for prayer groups. There *are* ways both to prevent major disagreements from arising and to handle them if they do arise.

The first step is to understand what kinds of problems most often tend to escalate into divisive disagreements.

A weakness that underlies almost all major disagreements is the group's lack of a common understanding of who they are and what they are about — in short, a lack of identity. In many groups, if you were to interview the members individually, you would find vastly different conceptions of what the group is and what it is supposed to be doing as it follows the Lord. Often this lack of clarity regarding purpose and expectation extends to the leaders of the group. This lack of common vision, of shared expectations, is the seedbed for almost all major disagreements.

There are particular areas in which confusion about group identity commonly leads to disagreement and division.

Structure. This applies both to the group's internal structure and to its relationships with outside institutions.

Internally, some members of the group consider well-established service teams and procedures a necessity, while others prefer a looser arrangement. Some prefer a structured prayer meeting, others expect a higher degree of spontaneity.

Questions of outside relationships have to do mainly with the parish and with other prayer groups. Is the prayer group an official parish organization under the direct guidance of the pastor and parish council, or is it simply an informal association not tied to parish structures? What kinds of relationships does it have with other prayer groups, with regional service centers, with nearby covenant communities?

Level of Commitment. Some will think of the weekly prayer meeting as one of many beneficial activities in their lives. They will feel pressured if other members assume that the group's goal is to become a Christian community and thus press for the establishment of growth groups that meet on other evenings, of a core group within the larger prayer group, of covenanted relationships.

Leadership. The questions are many. Who should lead? Who should not? Should the pastor of the parish be considered the leader of the group? Should priests be considered for leadership at all? Should laymen be considered at all? What about women?

How are leaders selected? What if it seems that a particular leader should be replaced? How much authority do leaders of the group have? On what basis do they exercise it?

Ecumenism. This can be a very difficult area. Typically, Catholic prayer groups find themselves divided into two groups: those who think the group should be openly and explicitly Catholic and those who think it should be distinctly ecumenical.

The first group may have strong feelings in favor of expressions of Marian piety, celebration of the eucharist as part of the prayer meeting, and so on. The second group will insist on setting aside those areas in which Christians disagree, for the sake of unity.

In many of these areas, there are no right or wrong approaches that apply to all groups in all places at all times. An individual prayer group has open to it a vast array of options regarding its structure and identity, any combination of which might be workable. The group must diligently seek God's mind about which options he wants it to adopt.

It is seldom the case that these differences of expectation are explicit, at least not at first. Most of them bubble below the surface, never mentioned, their existence sometimes not even realized. They appear only when they erupt.

All this suggests an obvious lesson: a prayer group should take some pains to clearly develop its identity. This means making sure that the expectations of the members are brought into the open and accounted for, so that everyone can share a common vision of what the group is and where it is going.

Even attempting this process, however, can lead to trouble. Many prayer groups lack some elements that would make it possible for them to discuss their identity in a peaceful, productive way. It is the lack of these same elements which makes it difficult to deal with divisive issues that do arise.

What are some of these elements? What are some things prayer groups must do now to avoid serious problems later?

Relationships. Most prayer groups pay far too little attention to building solid Christian personal relationships among members. "If a prayer group doesn't have a vision for the character of Christian relationships, a set of explicitly understood standards for how

Christians are supposed to behave in key situations, then it's all up for grabs," says Gabe Meyer, a leader in the charismatic renewal from Los Angeles.

It is easy for prayer groups to expend so much energy keeping the weekly prayer meeting going and organizing services and activities that developing their relationships as brothers and sisters in the Lord takes the back seat. But that order of priority is backwards.

Most disagreements either stem from relationship problems or are exacerbated by them. Jack Brombach, a leader from Minneapolis, finds that in divisive disagreements "there is usually a failure to recognize underlying relationship difficulties. Consequently, issues are dealt with on a superficial level."

The key to developing Christian relationships is to provide teaching on the subject. Many of us actually know very little about what Scripture teaches concerning committed love, loyalty, righteous speech, expressing affection, repairing wrongdoing—vital "skills" that give flesh and blood to the concept of *agape*.

There are books, tape sets, and magazine articles available that discuss these areas. I recommend that prayer groups make it a point to obtain these materials and present their teaching in a conscientious way.

The next step, of course, is application: finding ways to incarnate the principles in our daily lives. Fr. Brendan Murray, a leader from Convent Station, New Jersey, describes this as "creating and *living in* an environment of trust: trusting God, trusting one another, trusting the leadership group. Loyalty is the key factor in this."

Leadership. Another fundamental element is good leadership. Specifically this means leaders who have both the trust of the group and the authority to address problems that arise and steer the group to a successful resolution.

It is important that the leaders be in a position to take the reins and *lead*, not merely to "coordinate" or "facilitate" a nebulously defined consensus approach.

"In a group that lacks clear leadership," Jack Brombach says, "there is a tendency among the leaders to become overly spiritual and wait on the Lord for everything. Then when issues arise, the group is vulnerable to division."

A few simple steps can help a group of leaders function effectively:

1. There should be a clear acknowledgment of leadership in the prayer group. Everyone (especially the leaders!) should know who the leaders are and what their sphere of authority is. Those in leadership should be able to frankly and willingly accept their role.

Note the plural: leaders. Groups that have only one leader are more vulnerable to divisive disagreement than groups with shared leadership.

2. Leadership should not be exercised in a haphazard, off-the-cuff way. One simple aid: leaders should set a regular time to meet and develop an agenda that allows for both recurring and spontaneous matters. This helps insure that problems are handled as routine matters, not as crises.

3. Leaders should be especially vigilant to maintain their personal relationships with one another. A prayer group whose leaders can be easily divided is prey to divisive disagreement.

Plan Ahead. A third foundational element to prevent issues from becoming divisive is to develop a plan for how the group will handle differences of opinion when they arise.

I say, *"when* they arise," not, *"if* they arise." As a prayer group moves to clarify its goals and identity, it can expect that members will have ideas about how key areas should be approached, and that these ideas will not mesh perfectly.

"We should expect," Gabe Meyer says, "That disagreement and discussion ought to happen as a matter of course among any group of people." Many prayer groups, he says, are afraid of disagreement and either pretend it isn't there or overlook it when it does arise.

Some disagreement is not only inevitable but even healthy. What is crucial is not that differences never arise but that they be handled well when they do. Dealing with issues can be a source of growth and strength rather than of discord and division.

Kerry Koller, a leader from South Bend, Indiana, agrees. "One thing I often encounter," he says, "is not division but the problem of wanting to avoid division by not doing anything. No one wants to rock the boat, so nobody does anything. No new initiatives are taken, no new directions are sought, no new goals established. What happens is that everyone loses heart, their hope and faith erode, and they become aimless. There's really such a thing as a problem of not having enough disagreement, in the sense that no one is willing to try to move things forward.

"People shouldn't be afraid of disagreements," Koller says. "Confront them, deal with them, and move on past them. Letting them simmer only leads to more trouble in the end."

What should go into a plan for handling disagreement? Or to put the question from another perspective, what do you do when a major disagreement has already arisen?

The key element is communication. "The best way to deal with a potentially divisive issue," Kerry Koller says, "is to bring it into the open as soon as it's spotted. Seek input from the group. Find out what people are thinking. Keep all the channels open. Stress that you want to hear what others have to say."

The main responsibility for maintaining effective communication lies with the leaders. "People need to feel confident that the leaders have heard them. Not necessarily that the leaders are going to do everything they've suggested, but that their suggestions have been listened to, are being weighed, and will be responded to in some way."

Here are some steps that could be taken in handling a potentially divisive issue that has arisen.

1. Face it squarely. Problems thrive on neglect. To put it another way: the longer a disagreement is allowed to simmer, the hotter it gets. Leaders should decide that when a disagreement arises they will resolve it, not side-step it.

2. Bring complaints to the leaders. This is a basic principle of Christian relationships. Any time we see a problem requiring attention, we should speak to whoever has responsibility for the area and, consequently, the ability to deal with it. In a prayer group this is the leaders' team. We should specifically not "make our case" to others in the group who are not in a position to resolve the problem.

At the same time, the leaders should take steps to insure that they have heard from everyone who should be heard. Those who have not approached the leaders on their own should be sought out.

3. Don't form factions. Many times we approach disagreements on the basis of secular models of conflict. "One of the things that keeps issues going," Kerry Koller notes, "is the fact that people align themselves with a person who has a problem," even if that problem would not otherwise have concerned them.

Conversely, a person initiating discussion of a problem can consciously or unconsciously "recruit" other members to his "cause." "They think things operate in terms of party lines," Koller says, "and decide to force the leadership into accepting their position through political force. I call it spiritual blackmail: 'If you don't do it this way, we're all leaving.' "

Two simple principles apply here. First, make *your* complaints *yourself*; don't draw uninvolved people into them. Second, don't inject yourself into a situation that need not concern you.

4. Resolve the problem in the leaders' group. The leaders are the ones responsible for the prayer group. Ideally it should be possible for them, if they have done their homework in consulting group members, to resolve the issue among themselves and to develop an approach the whole group can accept. This is where good relationships among leaders, and trust and loyalty on the part of the whole group, pay off.

5. Discuss the problem with the whole group. Note that this is not the first step — a common misconception. By this time, all relevant input should have been given and received, so that there is no need for a general debate, which can easily become destructive in itself.

Rather, the leaders should be in a position to present the issues involved, describe the solution they think is called for, and help the group accept and implement their solution.

Again, it is important that everyone be heard out. It may be that the leaders will find it advisable to go back to the drawing board and modify their recommendations. This is a process that can easily be repeated if necessary.

In holding such a group session, it is important to explain clearly at the outset what are the goals and ground rules of the meeting, in order to avoid confusion and divisive debate.

6. Seek outside help. Many times it is valuable to seek wisdom and guidance from a more mature group. Many prayer groups have the kinds of relationships with other groups in their area that would make this possible if the need arose. Groups who have not established such relationships should consider doing so.

Fr. Michael Scanlan, former chairman of the National Service Committee, thinks that "every prayer group should have some kind of relationship with another group — ideally a larger, more mature prayer group or a covenant community or an area renewal center — someone who can be called on when problems come up."

Many problems can be solved internally if proper steps are followed. When it is necessary to seek outside help, we should be sure that the group we consult is respected and trusted by everyone involved. Also, it is the leaders who should initiate the process.

7. Trust the Lord. This, of course, should be done throughout the process, not only as a last resort. If everyone is committed to doing God's will and to seeking his solution, not their own, the power of the Holy Spirit can work freely to resolve differences and restore unity.

CHAPTER FOURTEEN

LET'S TALK ABOUT OUR DIFFERENCES

Michael Scanlan

I'VE been amazed, over the years, to find out how poorly business discussions among Christians can go sometimes. In team meetings and committee meetings, in planning and evaluation sessions, the people who ought to be able to have the most loving, fruitful, Spirit-filled discussions often have rather destructive and chaotic ones. Arguments crop up, people leave feeling guilty or ignored, issues are left hanging.

In some ways, we're conditioned to act that way. Our culture values controversy, argument, competition. We can see it in the way political campaigns are conducted, in the way government and business decisions are made, in our books, our movies, our television shows. I call it "hand-to-hand combat within Roberts' Rules of Order."

Much of the service we perform in our prayer groups and communities includes meetings and discussions. Therefore it's important that we develop a proper, Christian approach to this area. Consider four approaches that can undermine a discussion.

1. *Rivalry and Competition.* This is the attitude that says, "There's going to be a winner and a loser in this discussion, and I had better be on the winning team."

This is what Paul calls "party spirit" (Gal. 5:20, *RSV*). I remember wondering for years, what does Paul have against parties? Then I saw that party spirit is truly divisive. We are taught, as part of the democratic process, to identify ourselves with pressure groups or interest groups. All too quickly we label others, and say that we are for this and they are for that. As soon as we use "we-they" language, we are introducing division and mistrust.

2. *Double-mindedness*. By this I mean doing one thing while appearing to do another, through use of indirection and innuendo. I will give examples of four types of double-mindedness.

The first is the rhetorical question. We ask a question which is not really a question at all, but a statement — and one for which we are not held responsible, because we have hidden it in the question. A rhetorical question that we might hear in Christian discussion would be, "When are we going to receive support for all the hard work we're doing?" That's not really a question. It's a declaratory statement: "You are not supporting us." What should have been said was, "It seems to us that you are not supporting us as you should be." This is a statement that can be acted upon. Rhetorical questions bring in confusion, fog the issues, stalemate the situation, and frustrate people.

Double-mindedness also occurs when feelings of hurt are expressed in a way that implies a need for action, but fails to give the group a basis to act on: "Many people feel hurt and rejected and need support." The expression of such feelings can be encouraged as long as it is positive, recommends some kind of remedy so that the body of Christ can be built up. Feelings are not, in themselves, evil, and they should be expressed — but not in a way that imprisons a situation.

A third kind of double-mindedness is general implication of wrongdoing. We've seen this operating in political campaigns: "He's part of the Watergate group." This is a way of saying someone is dishonest, without being held accountable for saying so — implying guilt without actually dealing with the facts. In Christian settings, we might hear people say things like, "I think the Lord wants to deal with the pride present in this room," or, "I think we should stop worrying about ourselves and begin to love others." It is difficult to move forward under such an indictment.

A fourth area of double-mindedness is calling for repentance in a manner that actually states an opinion or makes an accusation. For instance, someone prays "that the Lord will overcome the hardheartedness of the leaders," or "for the sins we have committed in not being more respectful of theologians." A person may read a Scripture verse such as Matthew 23:13, "Woe to you, scribes and Pharisees, hypocrites," just after someone has preached a sermon or given an admonition.

3. *Accusation of Wrongdoing.* The least common is *direct* accusation; for example, "I accuse so-and-so of stealing from our conference collection." We find a way to deal with this in the gospels: we should confront any party who has injured us, directly and privately (Matt. 18:15-17).

Unfortunately, direct accusation is not as prevalent as the use of accusatory words which make statements of position; for example, making passing reference to the "tyranny" of the leaders, or the group's "indifference" to children. This approach simply assumes that someone has done something wrong, but does not deal with facts.

4. *Self-appointed Mediator.* This is what I call the gratuitous proxy. He speaks for one or more people present whose names he refuses to mention. He says they have been wronged and are hurt.

But when he gets through speaking, nobody can do anything—though some leaders, unfortunately, try. We can't do anything because we don't have the facts and names we need to begin reconciliation. We're stalemated. The self-appointed mediator sometimes acts out of a noble motive, and his statements are often accepted—and even lauded—in many of our assemblies. But such an approach undermines relationships.

Now let's consider four approaches that foster a Christian discussion, that help to build up the body of Christ.

1. *Brothers and Sisters in the Lord.* We need to acknowledge that we are seeking wisdom from the Lord, that we are seeking his plan, his answer, and are not coming with our own ideas to beat down somebody else.

As we expressly acknowledge our relationship as brothers and sisters in the Lord, we should see ourselves as servants of one another. "Do nothing from selfishness or empty conceit, but with humility of mind let each of you regard one another as more important than himself; do not merely look out for your own personal interests, but also for the interests of others." (Phil. 2:3,*NASB*).

Also, we must not presume dishonest motives on the part of other people. "Do not speak evil against one another, brethren. He that speaks evil against a brother or judges his brother, speaks evil against the law" (James 4:11).

2. *Be Direct.* Say what you mean. Don't avoid the real issue. Don't be hindered by feeling that your speech might not be sufficiently pious or erudite; just be direct. Say yes if you mean yes and no if you mean no.

3. *Be Precise.* Make your point in a way that allows people to respond. People frequently feel passed over when no one says anything in reply after they speak. If you are looking for some response, it is a good practice to ask a specific question at the end of your comments: "I would like to know whether anyone agrees with me," or, "I would like to know whether people disagree with me," or, "I would like to know whether anyone can supply the answers that I do not have."

It is best to make one point at a time when you speak. There may be various aspects of that one point; but make one point and trust the brothers and sisters to let you speak again to make another point later. Frequently, we feel we have to give our whole apologia at once, because we may not get the floor again. But when we finish, everyone is confused as to what we have said, or they remember only a little here and there. Little wonder we are more apt to feel unsupported and unheard in such a situation.

4. *Submit to Headship.* The chairman should have the authority to preserve order, to call on those who wish to speak, to decide time limits, and to determine what will be handled first. Secondly, the chairman should have the authority to clarify statements, to ask the speaker questions, and to rephrase statements.

Discussions should be free and open. They will be if we express our relationship as brothers and sisters in the Lord and approach discussions in a way that is precise and ordered under headship. It is difficult to find anything that takes priority over our relating to one another as brothers and sisters in open, stable, solid ways. Therefore, a Christian discussion should build up those relationships.

We may not agree or have one mind on all the issues, but we must learn that we can see things very differently from one another and still be the body of Jesus Christ and true servants of him and one another.

III.

Before and After

Much of what a prayer group does takes place outside the weekly prayer meeting. Its members teach one another, pray for and with one another, support one another. And they share with others God's gift of new life in the Spirit.

CHAPTER FIFTEEN

BASIC CHRISTIAN INSTRUCTION

Bruce Yocum

WHEN people give their lives to Jesus, they don't automatically learn how to stop living in un-Christian ways and how to start living under his lordship. Usually, they're faced with a number of basic, practical questions: "How should I pray?" "What is a Christian supposed to do when he gets angry with someone?" "How can I get along better with my boss?"

People need teaching on what Christian life is, how it differs from the life of the world, and how they can go about living it day by day. Unfortunately, few of our groups do an adequate job of providing this kind of teaching, which we might call basic instruction, because most of us don't fully appreciate the important role it should play in our lives.

It's important to distinguish basic instruction from some other kinds of Christian teaching. Often, talks at prayer meetings fall into one of two categories: "exhortation," which means trying to motivate people, or "teaching the mysteries," which means penetrating the deeper truths of the Christian faith. When someone gives an inspiring talk encouraging us to have greater zeal, that's an example of exhortation; when someone reflects on the nature of the Trinity or the symbolism of an obscure Scripture passage, that's teaching the mysteries.

Many of us tend to over-value these kinds of teaching, considering them rather more spiritual than other kinds. Yet we do well to ask ourselves whether they meet people's real needs. For example, understanding the Christian mysteries will be interesting but often not really helpful to most people. Their real problems are learning how to pray, how to read Scripture, how to recognize and be free of wrongdoing, how to relate with their husband or wife, how to get on top of their emotions. Similarly, it makes little sense to exhort people to live better Christian lives when they may not yet know *how* to go about doing it.

Basic instruction deals with the problems of how to live, day by day, as a Christian. It is not intended to teach the mysteries, or to convert people, or even to motivate them. The criterion for its success is whether or not it helps people understand how a Christian should act in his daily life. It may be very inspirational and insightful, but if it doesn't help people live the Christian life, then it isn't successful basic instruction.

The first step in providing basic instruction is determining what people's needs really are. There is a fairly simple way to do this; so simple, in fact, that it often doesn't occur to us: asking people what areas they need teaching in.

We have found this to be very helpful in our own community. After each of our basic instruction courses, people are asked to fill out an evaluation. One of the things the evaluation asks is, "Do you have any needs that haven't been met by any of the teaching offered in the community?"

The answers are revealing. In the several years since we began asking this question, we've very seldom had people say things like, "I need to know more theology." The concerns they have are always very practical and very personal: "I've got a bad temper that I haven't learned to control." "The other people at my office aren't Christian and I can't seem to get along with them." For prayer group leaders, the simple act of asking people what their problems are will help a great deal in determining what topics should be covered by basic instruction.

Once we've determined what people's needs are, the next step is to figure out what to tell them. We ourselves may not know the solutions to people's problems; in fact, we may be facing similar problems ourselves. For most groups, the easiest approach will be to take advantage of the many basic instruction courses available on cassette tape. Groups can listen to the tapes and discuss them together, or the group's leaders can adapt the material and give the talks themselves.

There are a number of things to keep in mind when presenting basic instruction.

First, it shouldn't be too theoretical. It should be practical. We should include theory only to set a context for the practical-down-to-earth advice we really want to communicate. There is certainly a place for theoretical contemplation in the Christian life, but that place is not in basic instruction. When we teach people how to live the Christian life, we shouldn't do it in a highly theoretical way; that just doesn't help them very much.

Second, it should be presented in a way that people can identify with. When we talk about something, we should do it in such a way that people can say, "I know just what he means; that's just the kind of thing that happens to me." When we reach people at that level, they'll be able to receive and apply the teaching we give them more thoroughly.

For example, a talk on the importance of prayer could be given in a number of ways. We might present a long list of theoretical ruminations on the nature of prayer, the union of the soul with God, or the various prayer techniques that have been used by Christians throughout history. People might find a talk like that interesting, maybe even inspiring; but chances are it wouldn't help them much in getting their own prayer life to work right. It's too theoretical.

Or we could decide to make our thoughts on prayer more concrete by speaking on how to pray when we're alone in the Andes mountains. We could give all kinds of concrete, specific advice — not a speck of theory — but it still wouldn't help people much. Most of our listeners will never be alone in the Andes. They can't identify with that experience at all. Most of them are going to school, working, or taking care of a house and children. If we want to help them with their prayer lives, we have to talk about "How to pray when the phone is ringing continually," or "How to pray with three children in the house," or "How to fit a daily prayer time into an eight-hour work day."

Since basic instruction is not usually effective when presented during a prayer meeting, groups might want to establish special "foundations" or "growth" courses to be conducted just before or after the weekly prayer meeting. Such courses would be available to people who have been baptized in the Spirit and who are ready to learn more about Christian living.

Prayer groups and communities should seriously consider making some kind of basic instruction available to their members. In many groups, this will mean giving basic instruction priority over other kinds of teaching. But it's well worth our time and energy. Helping people learn how to conduct themselves as Christians in all their daily activities should be one of our primary concerns.

CHAPTER SIXTEEN

PRAYER ROOMS

Ann Thérèse Shields

M ANY groups have adopted the practice of having a "prayer room" after their regular prayer meetings, in order to pray with people for special needs. Such ministry is often confusing and frustrating, both to those ministering and to those receiving ministry. Those leading the prayer room are often unnecessarily worn and spent at the end of the session. Those being prayed with often leave frustrated or hurt because of unmet needs.

Much of this confusion arises from unclear expectations and undefined limits for the ministry. Let us first, then, examine what prayer room ministry is not, then clarify what it is, and discuss who should take part in it and how it should be done.

First, prayer room ministry is separate from deliverance ministry. People often come to a prayer room simply to be freed from relatively minor spiritual oppression or "hassling" in some area. Such prayer *can* be handled by the prayer room. But deliverance prayer for those who need freedom from bondage to a particular sin or habit should be done at a different time and place, and only by those trained, gifted, and set aside for this service by the leaders of the prayer group.

Second, the prayer room is not the appropriate place to pray for those not present. If an individual has a family member or friend who is ill, he or she should simply ask other prayer group members to intercede for that person during the week.

Finally, the prayer room is not the place for extensive counseling. If persons who are obviously burdened by some psychological problem come for prayer, it is essential to ask some important questions:

— Is the group equipped with a counseling ministry to handle such needs?

— Is the person sufficiently committed to the group that such counseling and follow-up, if available, would be fruitful?

— Does the group have a means of referral to professionally trained persons when necessary? Do not allow persons to labor under the expectation that you or your group can meet their needs if, in fact, you are not equipped to do so.

The kinds of needs which *can* be met by the prayer room ministry include:

1. *Physical.* Any illness for which people seek prayer for healing.

2. *Spiritual.* During the prayer meeting people often feel that the Holy Spirit is pointing out an area in their lives not yet under the lordship of Jesus. Prayer to help them surrender that area to the Lord not only serves that person but builds the whole body.

(If the group is Catholic, making the sacrament of reconciliation available after the prayer meeting can be an effective means to new life and spiritual healing.)

3. *Emotional.* Often, people are burdened by anxiety, tension, frustration, or anger over a particular situation. They need prayer for wisdom, courage, and strength to be able to respond to the situation as a Christian. Keeping the vision of the Lord before their eyes at this time can encourage and strengthen them.

If people come for prayer week after week when they actually need counseling, we are not serving them by continual prayer. The problem can only be compounded through overspiritualization and false dependency. Be truthful. Tell them in a simple, loving way what you believe they need to do. Either refer them to the proper ministry within the prayer group or direct them to seek professional help from outside sources.

There are also people who do not need counseling but nevertheless go for prayer to a number of persons, including the prayer room team members, in the course of a week. Such people have an unmet need for attention and request prayer as a means to receive it. In addition, seeking prayer is often a means of deferring action on something an individual needs to do. If such patterns continue, these people will not grow and those trying to help will be drained.

Leaders of prayer groups who select people to serve in a prayer room should first seek those whose lives of prayer are bearing fruit, those to whom the members of the prayer group already turn for the power and fruit of their prayer.

Second, leaders should look for men and women with discernment, compassion, wisdom, and common sense. They should also be:

—sensitive listeners, who can hear what is really being said
—skilled at questioning, so that the heart of what to pray for can be determined quickly
—trustworthy, able to maintain confidentiality
—free of serious personal problems.

It is important that those serving in the prayer room be an established team. A rotation system, or simply asking those who happen to be free on a given night to serve, does not bring about unity of purpose and direction within the ministry.

Once the team is chosen—the size being determined according to the average number of people requesting prayer—leaders of the prayer group should appoint someone to take charge of the team's activities.

A few simple procedures will help the prayer room function effectively:

—The team members must be reconciled to one another at all times. If there is dissension, the full power of God's love can be limited, and witness to the body seriously threatened. Reconciliation, therefore, must take place before ministry begins.

—There should be a time of prayer for wisdom prior to ministry. It is ideal to delay the start of the prayer room for ten minutes after the conclusion of the prayer meeting. This allows sufficient time for the team to move to the prayer room and pray before the others arrive.

— Team members, as far as possible, should pray in pairs. In this way, mutual support and discernment are available, and the time required for prayer is considerably reduced.

— The leader should be free to circulate among those praying with people, to give support and discernment where necessary, and to intercede for all involved during the actual time of prayer.

— A brief time of prayer for refreshment and peace should be held at the conclusion of the session.

— During the week, team members should be committed to intercede for each other and for those with whom they have prayed.

If clear decisions are made in advance as to what areas the prayer room ministry will handle, if those with the appropriate gifts are selected to serve, and if team members maintain a deep unity among themselves, the prayer room can be a powerful instrument of healing and growth for the whole prayer group.

CHAPTER SEVENTEEN

EVANGELISM

Larry Alberts

WHEN God decided to act in power through the charismatic renewal, many of us found ourselves sovereignly baptized in the Spirit, speaking in tongues, and following the Lord as never before. He was real to us, manifestly active in our lives. Prayer groups emerged all around the world as we began to worship God together.

We soon found that praising and worshipping God was only part of his purpose for our prayer groups. He also wanted us to build his body on earth. Something special about the New Testament church caught our attention: "And the Lord added to their number day by day those who were being saved" (Acts 2:47, RSV). The Lord was calling us to imitate this pattern as we welcomed others into our new life with him. We understood that Jesus himself had instructed us to do this in his great commission. "Go therefore and make disciples of all nations" (Matt. 28:19). Evangelism — sharing the good news of Jesus — is the key to this.

How were we to go about it? Some said, "All we need to do is pray and God will send the right people to us." But even Paul, powerful in prayer, a worthy example, and inherently persuasive, was conscious that he had to be a skilled master builder. He cautioned God's ministers in Corinth: "Let each man take care how he builds" (1 Cor. 3:10).

We've seen that some prayer groups don't last. In many cases, weak evangelism is a major cause of the difficulty. Like Paul, we need the wisdom, time, energy, and love which, with prayer and God's grace, make evangelism effective.

Since early in the charismatic renewal some helpful structures have been developed, including leaders' teams, explanation rooms, Life in the Spirit Seminars, and open meetings. We've also gained wisdom about how prayer groups can practice effective evangelism. In general the leaders of a prayer group are responsible for overseeing the group's evangelistic outreach.

Open prayer meetings are a prime opportunity to evangelize. Besides prayer and worship, short, simple teachings and prepared sharings and testimonies should be a normal part of our open meetings.

The teaching and sharing at prayer meetings should contribute to an accurate view of Christianity. For example, God isn't a means to our own end. God created us to love and serve him. Though we all come to the Lord with needs, it is not enough to have people come to the Lord simply to get their problems solved and their needs met. The prayer meeting leaders should help others see Christianity as a high ideal so that men and women of high integrity and character, men and women seeking high ideals, can embrace Christianity. In other words, people need to know that they are committing themselves to a worthy cause. This will attract strong people who might not be drawn to the Lord simply on the basis of having their needs met, people who in fact have much to give.

What goes on before and after the meeting is often as important as what happens during the meeting. We should be careful not to leave people standing around alone at these times. Everyone should be encouraged to take an active responsibility for new people, especially through informal socializing. Members of the prayer group should greet new people, introduce themselves, and help them feel at ease. Welcoming people is just common courtesy; it is also a vital part of helping people come to the Lord.

It is good to try to spend time with people in situations that are less formal than prayer meetings. We can invite them out for coffee after the meeting or have them over for dinner. It is important for people to see us in situations other than prayer. We can and should create ways for this to happen. We should be willing to look for common interests, then go the extra mile so that others can be brought into our life.

An explanation before the open meeting will set new people at ease and help them understand the order of the meeting. In addition, it is an excellent opportunity to declare the good news. The people leading the explanation room must appreciate its role and importance. They must be properly motivated to serve new people and be able to put others at ease so that newcomers can raise questions and express themselves openly.

While the explanation room can do a certain amount to orient new people, it is everyone's responsibility to reach out to new people and love them.

Not everyone, however, is equally gifted or should be equally involved in evangelistic work. There may be people in the group, for example, who have a special gift for evangelism. They should be found and placed in situations where they can be most effective. Leaders should see that these people get special encouragement and training.

Some people in the prayer group should not be engaging in active evangelism because their lives do not yet conform to the Christian message. When their lives clearly demonstrate that they are a new creation in Christ, their speech will be more convincing. Then they can speak more freely on the Lord's behalf.

But the desire to bring others into the life of Christ should be in the hearts of all Christians. Evangelism isn't something that people can do only after years of practice or studying special techniques, nor does it require extraordinary holiness. It is something that God is expecting us to do as a normal part of daily life, especially when our life is in good order. While leaders need to caution people with severe problems, it is even more important to encourage and support most of the people in the group to witness.

Of course some of us are over-enthusiastic about leading people to the Lord. We can overwhelm newcomers and turn them off. We appear to be walking computers of biblical information, puffed up with high-power testimony. The effect of this approach is often more damaging than constructive.

When I first came to the Lord, I was so convinced of God's goodness and his love for me and for all men that I was obsessed with leading every person I met to him. Though I led many people to Christ, there were probably many more that I became an obstacle for.

The Lord began to show me that while zeal and enthusiasm were important, his wisdom was even more important. The Lord continued to show me that I needed to grow in wisdom and in love. And the more I loved the people I was witnessing to, the more the Lord would lead them to himself. Instead of coming on strong, the Lord wanted me to simply tell my story — how he had acted in my life and how much I had experienced his love. Most people don't need to be preached to or judged, they need to experience care and concern.

Loving people and growing in wisdom involve becoming sensitive to God's timing. As a child on a New York farm, I learned early that pruning fruit trees during the wrong season was injurious. The sap would flow from any sizeable cut and the "bleeding" often rotted parts of the tree. This principle applies to premature evangelism. However well-intentioned we are, we must exercise care not to do God's work "out of season." Over the years I've become more patient with God's timetable for working in others. So often he has reminded me, "You love them; I'll save them."

There are many methods of evangelism. Some of us are more familiar with approaches like the four spiritual laws often used in explanation rooms, others with discussions over coffee, or still others with street corner encounters. Whatever the method, it is essential to be as natural as possible when evangelizing. Be yourself, and let the other person do likewise.

Even as we grow in practical wisdom about how to share the good news with others, we must relax and trust the Lord to bring forth the fruit. We want people to join the Lord's cause, not our cause. The Lord's cause is true. It is the most worthy reason for living. Other people can best believe that truth if they can see its reality in our lives. We should not communicate it to them as something that is abstract or removed from our normal life-style.

It is easier for them to receive from us if we approach them as friends and not as people that we are out to convert.

Jesus functioned best in natural circumstances. The calling of the disciples, the conversion of the woman at the well, the encounter with Zacchaeus, the many times Jesus healed people, even the last supper, all happened in ordinary times and places. Sharing meals together, having people drop by our homes, and hosting parties are all effective ways of communicating the practicality of our faith, because in these situations we are most easily sharing ourselves.

We should also be open to the promptings and inspirations of the Spirit when we evangelize. Praying before we talk with a person helps us to be tuned in to these things. The Lord often reveals questions he wants us to ask or things he'd like us to talk about. Peter and Cornelius were both prepared by the Lord in advance to receive each other (see Acts 10). This is a good example of how direction through revelation allows the impossible to happen. In any case, the Lord wants us to be gracious as we share his life, and to rely on him to change the hearts of men and women.

Finally, I'd like to mention a problem many of us have faced concerning the place of spiritual gifts in evangelism. When I first became involved with a prayer group about six years ago, we suffered from what I would call confused identity. Some were strongly in favor of spiritual gifts and some were strongly opposed. So we took a middle-of-the-road position in an attempt to please everyone. We soon saw our mistake. Since we didn't want to offend anyone, we didn't teach clearly about the charismatic gifts. They became almost nonexistent. Then the Lord gave us a new understanding about the use of spiritual gifts.

Because the display of the Spirit's gifts is extraordinary, it attracts onlookers. We began teaching clearly about spiritual gifts and more people began to exercise more gifts. We noticed that when the gifts were exercised, faith increased, our prayer deepened, and love abounded. The gifts of the Spirit alone don't always lead to changed lives. The gifts should foster the fruit of the Spirit which will have a greater impact on new people.

We found that even though some new people were unimpressed with the gifts of the Spirit, many would testify to how they were overwhelmed by the love seen among us. The gifts they could deny or reject, but the fruits of love, joy, and peace were irresistible. Because the gifts of the Spirit attracted new people and fostered greater love in the group, clearly establishing our identity as a charismatic prayer group made a significant difference.

Although not everyone has a powerful ministry of evangelism which leads thousands of people to the Lord, all of us are called to witness to Jesus Christ. Jesus equips us as individuals and as prayer groups with the fruit of the Spirit so that we can lead people into his kingdom. The power of God is the life and character of Jesus revealed among us. Let it be said of us that by "praising God and having favor with all the people," the Lord "added to their number day by day those who were being saved" (Acts 2:47).

CHAPTER EIGHTEEN

DELIVERANCE

Randy Cirner

O NE of the most difficult areas for prayer groups to deal with is deliverance. This is not surprising, since most groups suffer from a lack of proper understanding of deliverance. Sensationalist stories in the media and bad experiences only add to the problem. For example, a movie like *The Exorcist* can be a source of fears about the devil.

Even so, I don't think secular books and movies such as *The Exorcist* have had nearly as much effect on prayer groups as material coming out of the Christian sector. From one end of the Christian spectrum we hear that the devil is not a personal being at all. He is, rather, the impersonal projection of human sins and weakness. Casting out such "demons" is merely an exercise in psychological catharsis.

On the other hand, much Christian literature portrays demons as the immediate cause of virtually all of our sins, weaknesses, and bad experiences. Deliverance, as described in this literature, is dramatic. The demons come out coughing, spitting, vomiting, screaming, or producing some other terrifying manifestation. In some instances this literature portrays the person performing the deliverance as having final and authoritative discernment about which demons may be present.

Also, many prayer groups have come in contact with persons who claim to have a deliverance ministry, or centers that specialize in deliverance. Some of these people have received a unique gift from the Lord and perform a valuable service. But all too often, unsuspecting prayer group members find themselves in a situation where histrionics and emotion are mistaken for the action of God. Experiences of this sort quickly sour people's attitude toward deliverance.

As a result of these kinds of things, most prayer groups simply avoid deliverance. This avoidance isn't always based on fear alone. Prayer group leaders understand that they have a responsibility to protect the group from teachings and actions which will cause confusion. Further, leaders do not feel equipped to handle deliverance, and are hesitant to get their prayer group involved in something they can't direct adequately.

Before discussing practical aspects of deliverance, some basic distinctions must be made. First of all, it is important to recognize that all Christians are involved in personal spiritual warfare.

"Be sober, be watchful. Your adversary the devil prowls around like a roaring lion, seeking some one to devour. Resist him, firm in your faith, knowing that the same experience of suffering is required of your brotherhood throughout the world" (1 Pet. 5:8-9, *RSV*). Peter tells his readers that all Christians need to fight a battle with the adversary. Each person must resist the devil's influence in his own life.

In order to do this effectively, a Christian needs to know how to recognize and deal with a direct attack by evil spirits. Prayer groups can and should provide themselves with the instruction necessary to repel satanic temptation and harassment (see *New Covenant*, April, May 1974; December 1977).

There is another level of spiritual warfare that is intended to free areas of a person's life from bondage to evil spirits. Usually this involves having other people with the necessary gifts and responsibility pray with a person. They help him take authority over the work of evil spirits in his life. This is the level of spiritual warfare I'm talking about when I use the term "deliverance."

Deliverance, in this sense, does not deal with severe cases of demonic influence such as possession. Identifying actual demonic possession is difficult, and casting out such demons is an arduous task requiring special gifts. (Some Christian churches have had a recognized office of exorcist to deal with such cases.)

Despite the many potential problems with deliverance, it is still an important tool for Christians. As with any tool, its effectiveness depends on our knowing how and when to use it. One general principle can be stated: prayer groups should not attempt deliverance unless they are solidly committed, have recognized leaders who can give direction to the group members, and can provide sufficient pastoral care to handle "follow-up" with people who have been prayed with.

The following guidelines are intended to help prayer groups determine whether they are able to make use of deliverance and, if so, how to begin.

1. *Deliverance should take place in the context of overall pastoral care.* Prayer groups should see deliverance as a pastoral tool enabling the leaders to care for the group and lead people to a deeper relationship with the Lord.

During deliverance, it is important for those doing the praying to have personal and pastoral knowledge of the person they are praying with. Because deliverance touches personal areas, it is important that the person being prayed with trust those praying with him. The gifts of revelation and discernment which operate in the prayer session are not meant to substitute for the personal and pastoral knowledge, but to work with them to bring to the fore those areas in need of prayer. Deliverance sessions can also be a time for advice and counsel on how to continue to work on a particular area of sin or weakness.

Because of the pastoral nature of deliverance, the leaders of the prayer group should be the ones who conduct prayer for deliverance. The pastoral skill, knowledge, and confidentiality involved usually require that this area not be given over to other members of the prayer group.

There is a very clear implication in all this: If your prayer group does not have mature leadership, or if you have only loosely structured elements of commitment and responsibility, don't get into deliverance. Your prayer group does not have the necessary foundations for such a ministry.

2. *The leaders should come to a common mind about deliverance.* They should study the subject together and get their questions answered to a satisfactory degree. They should resolve any differences they may have. If the leadership is divided on whether to begin deliverance, they should wait until agreement is reached. Most important of all, the leaders should determine, through prayer and consultation, whether God wants the prayer group to make use of deliverance in its pastoral care.

The leaders should be prayed with for deliverance themselves before they attempt to pray with others in the prayer group. As well as being personally beneficial for the leaders, it will give them some good personal experience to work from.

3. *Get experienced help from outside the group.* Leaders ought not to think they have all the tools necessary to begin praying with people after reading one or two books about deliverance. A willing heart and two books under your belt are no substitute for supervised training. The leaders should look for help from mature, experienced people in another prayer group or community.

Where possible, I suggest that the leaders of the prayer group travel to another group that has a solid deliverance ministry and learn as much as they can from them. Spend time in their group. See the fruits of their prayers for deliverance. Get your questions answered. This is where the leaders themselves should be prayed with. When they return to their own prayer group, they should take time to evaluate their own experience.

A word of caution: seek help from a group you know to be solid, mature, experienced in deliverance. I know of very few groups who have such qualifications. Much confusion and turmoil can result from learning wrong things from immature or misdirected groups.

4. *Start slow and easy.* Give yourselves time to gain experience and confidence. If you run into difficulties and find yourselves in over your heads, admit the problem and stop.

Prayer for deliverance should be directed mainly toward the

more mature and stable members of the prayer group. It is a mistaken notion that deliverance should be aimed primarily at people with significant emotional and spiritual problems. It is true that, in the proper context, such people can derive great benefit from deliverance. But prayer groups normally should not try to handle such cases; they should work with Christians whose lives are in basic order but who are experiencing resistance in some areas of life.

Similarly, deliverance is for the prayer group, not for friends, relatives, or needy people in town. Prayer group leaders need to resist any temptation to become involved in deliverance outside the prayer group. Pray only with people for whom you have some direct and immediate pastoral responsibility.

Pray with people one at a time. Avoid any mass-deliverance sessions where you round up a bunch of people and start praying over them. As far as pastoral care is concerned, mass-deliverance sessions are not very helpful.

5. *Never force anyone to be prayed with.* At times, you may think that deliverance is just what a particular person needs. You may even be right. But if the person himself doesn't agree with you, you must not push him into it. At such times you should place the person in God's hands and pray that, if deliverance is really needed, God will help him see it.

6. *The leaders should make sure that deliverance is handled in an orderly and peaceful way.* They should decide who to pray with, and not let circumstances dictate. There are probably a number of people in your prayer group who think that deliverance is going to be the answer to their problems. They will want you to pray with them as soon as possible, and will keep after you until you yield. Leaders should not let such pressure set the agenda. Pray only with the people you feel right about praying with; God will take care of those you can't.

Leaders should exercise strong control over any outsiders who come to the prayer group claiming to have a ministry of deliverance. As mentioned before, itinerant ministries are difficult to assess accurately, and can cause harm in such personal areas as deliverance. No outside person should be allowed to pray with people in the group unless the leaders are confident in the person and his gift, and are willing to take the time to follow up with the people he prays with.

Prayer groups in the charismatic renewal should not be afraid of deliverance. At the same time, they should not feel that it is necessary to have such a ministry operating. If you have a mature prayer group able to handle deliverance, thank God for it and use the gift wisely.

The Lord wants each of his people to live as free a Christian life as possible. But even if a person never has an opportunity for deliverance, God's grace is still sufficient for him. In Ephesians 6:10-19, St. Paul puts spiritual warfare in its cosmic context. But he also gives some concrete advice on how an individual ought to fight in this battle. What Paul says can be boiled down to one simple idea: If you want to win in your fight against the devil, live an effective Christian life. Righteous living, knowledge and love of God, faith, and truth are the things that close the doors and defend the walls against Satan's activity.

Dealing with the devil through deliverance and exorcism is an important element in spiritual warfare. But the most important arena of battle is the Christian's daily struggle to love God and his brothers and sisters, to die to sin and the flesh, to overcome the world, and to resist Satan. These are the things that make dynamic Christian lives, strengthen prayer groups, and build the kingdom of God.

CHAPTER NINETEEN

PREPARING FOR DIFFICULT TIMES

George Kosicki

How should individuals, families, and prayer groups respond to the prophecies, given in the charismatic renewal over the past several years, telling of coming difficulties for the church and the world? I consider these prophecies as words of the Lord spoken to us because he loves us and wants to prepare us for a time of trial for the church and the world. His words are serious and they call for a serious response on our part. (See *New Covenant*, February 1978.)

This kind of word is not limited just to charismatic groups. Pope Paul VI has given vivid prophetic descriptions of the condition of the world, calling for our response. In this article I would like to outline the responses of Pope Paul and leaders of the charismatic renewal to the prophetic vision each has received.

During Pentecost 1975, Pope Paul spoke prophetically to the whole church about the condition of the world and the need to implore the Spirit for a new Pentecost:

"One must also recognize a prophetic intuition on the part of our predecessor John XXIII, who envisaged a kind of new Pentecost as a fruit of the council. We too have wished to place ourself in the same perspective and in the same attitude of expectation.

Not that Pentecost has ever ceased to be an actuality during the whole history of the church, but so great are the needs and the perils of the present age, so vast the horizons of mankind drawn toward world coexistence and powerless to achieve it, that there is no salvation for it except in a new outpouring of the gift of God. Let him then come, the Creating Spirit, to renew the face of the earth!" (*On Christian Joy*).

There is no salvation for this present age except in a new Pentecost. Therefore, implore the Spirit. This is the response and remedy of the leader of the Catholic Church.

In January 1976 and January 1977, leaders from around the United States, comprising the National Service Committee and its Advisory Committee, met at South Bend, Indiana. During these meetings the recent prophecies in the charismatic renewal were discussed in order to approach some common discernment on how to respond to them.

What I am presenting here as the response of charismatic leaders is taken from my notes of these meetings. Since then I've reflected on the notes, summarized them, made them my own, and shared them with many groups. I've also interpreted them and added to them my personal experience. I cannot give a detailed blueprint of steps to take. Only the Lord can lead us, a step at a time, as we listen to him and trust him.

Your strength is in your relationships with the Lord and with your brothers and sisters. In time of trial, your strength is in those you can trust.

In your relationship with the Lord, move with him into deeper repentance, deeper trust, and deeper surrender. He has so much more for you. Invite him to draw you more and more into the fire of his divine love. His desire is to be Lord and savior of every aspect of your life. Trust him in all circumstances because he is Lord of all. Thank him and praise him for all he is doing. The Lord is your light and salvation, whom shall you fear?

I interpret the raising of Lazarus as a lesson calling all of us to this total trust. "This sickness (this time of trial) is not to end in death; rather it is for God's glory, that through it the Son of God may be glorified" (John 11:4, NAB). Do you believe that even in the coming trials the Lord Jesus is the resurrection and the life?

Do you believe that even if you die you will rise with him? Jesus speaks to all of us. "Did I not assure you that if you believed you would see the glory of God displayed?" (John 11:40).

In your relationships with your brothers and sisters, move with the Lord. Get into the kind of relationship he has called you to and commit yourself to it. Deepen it with greater commitment, love, and forgiveness. Grow in this relationship by daily dying to yourself and to self-concern. There is no shortcut around this daily cross.

Your strength in times of trial will be in your relationships. Ask: "Lord, what relationships do you want me to be in?" Obey the call of the Lord and get into those relationships now. The Lord wants you to be strong in his body. His body may be your own family, a small cluster of families, your prayer group, a support group, your parish, or your community. The Lord has a place for you. Your strength is in being there now.

Your weakness, where you are vulnerable to attack, is in your personal life. It may be a strained relationship, a resentment, a habit of sin. Get the weakness in order by repentance, deliverance, and healing. The Lord is waiting for you to act in these areas. Submit them to him so that he can strengthen you.

You who are leaders: Because you are in a position of responsibility, it is you who are the most vulnerable to attack against your weaknesses, especially sensuality, resentment, jealousy, and pride. Humble yourselves that the Lord may exalt you. Protect one another, submit your shortcomings to one another, and help each other in the areas of your weakness.

Don't neglect your responsibilities to your brothers and sisters; rather, serve each other with love. "Whatever you do, work at it with your whole being. Do it for the Lord rather than for men, since you know full well you will receive an inheritance from him as your reward. Be slaves of Christ the Lord" (Col. 3:23-24).

Don't store up for yourselves a supply of goods and necessities for a further crisis, but "seek first his kingship over you, his way of holiness, and all these things will be given you besides. . . . Do not lay up for yourselves an earthly treasure. Moths and rust corrode; thieves break in and steal. Make it your practice instead to store up heavenly treasure, which neither moths nor rust corrode nor thieves break in and steal. Remember, where your treasure is, there your heart is also" (Matt. 6:33; 6:19-21).

Don't try to escape the coming trial by denying that it is coming; rather, prepare for the trial by vigilance and prayer. "As for the exact day or hour, no one knows it, neither the angels in heaven nor the Son, but the Father only. . . . Stay awake, therefore!" (Matt. 24:36, 42). "So be on the watch. Pray constantly for the strength to escape whatever is in prospect, and to stand secure before the Son of Man" (Luke 21:36).

During the time of trial we need to make these gospel attitudes our own:

1. *Be a servant of God's word and not of your own opinion.* God's word needs to be taught clearly and in the power of the Holy Spirit during times of confusion. Our own opinions, formed by secular currents of thought, will only add to the confusion. Our own opinions will not bring people to the Lord, but the living word of the Lord will bring people to him.

2. *Speak the truth in love (Eph. 4:15).* Both the church and the world need to hear the word of the Lord. The truth must be spoken in love and in all humility. We must ask for the courage to speak when a thousand dissonant voices clamor to be heard. Pray and study that you may know the truth and not speak out of ignorance. Ask the Lord for love, that you may not judge but rather intercede in love for those you see in error and darkness.

All three elements of speaking the truth in love are essential: We must *speak* and not be silent. We must *know* the truth and not be in error ourselves. And we must *love* those we speak to, and intercede for them.

3. *Test all things (1 Thess. 5:21).* We need to protect ourselves in times of confusion. One way to protect ourselves is to test all things according to a simple method of discernment. Ask yourself if this activity, this article, this relationship, this attitude, is leading you toward the Lord or away from him. Is it increasing your love, reverence, faith, and commitment to Jesus Christ and to his people? If not, stop and turn away. Do only what builds your love, reverence, faith, and commitment to the Lord Jesus and his church. Time is too short and too precious to be wasted.

4. *Be holy*. This is the call given to all of us: be filled and guided by the Holy Spirit; live, as it were, baptized in the Spirit. The call to holiness is a summary of all that the Lord wants of us in response to the prophecies.

If we respond to the prophecies in these radical ways we can expect to be persecuted. Our lives will be a witness of conviction that cannot be resisted. "Blest are those persecuted for holiness' sake; the reign of God is theirs" (Matt. 5:10).

These responses to the prophecies need to be developed by your own reflection, prayer, and sharing, in order to be put into practice.

Three words of encouragement keep coming to me: peace, patience, and perseverance. Be at peace, that is, be in right relationship with the Lord, with one another, and with yourself. Be patient for the Lord's perfect timing of events: "Love is patient" (1 Cor. 13:4). Be persevering in your commitment to the Lord and to your brothers and sisters. The Lord wants us to persevere in peaceful patience through all that he has made ready for those who love and obey him.

Finally, one key word is dominant with me: Intercede! Implore the Spirit! Ask the Lord to act in a sovereign way to renew the church. Intercede that the leaders of the church be stirred to call the church to repent and turn to the Lord in a radical way. The Lord is calling us now to unite with the whole church and the whole heavenly court and to cry out for a "new outpouring of the gift of God. Let him then come, the Creating Spirit, to renew the face of the earth!" (Paul VI, *On Christian Joy*).

IV.

Special Topics

As in other areas, there is some specialization among prayer groups. Some feel called to serve specific groups of people, perhaps teenagers or house-wives. Some find that particular services are needed to support the life of the group: book tables, songbooks, prayer lists. All can find their place in the master's plan.

CHAPTER TWENTY

TEEN PRAYER MEETINGS

Jim Brassil

JOYFUL song, spontaneous praise, deep awareness of the presence of the Lord, and secure peace characterize the teen prayer meeting. Everything focuses on Jesus, who is the center of it all. Hearing his name spoken with reverence and love gives one the clear conviction that Jesus is truly the friend of teenagers.

Some of those taking part in the prayer meeting have, for the first time in their lives, come into a deep awareness of Jesus' personal love for them. Many others have grown in depth and maturity in prayer. There is acceptance, belonging, togetherness, a true sense of family unity. There is no age barrier or class distinction; rather, there is respect and even reverence for one another. Those present at such a gathering are immediately aware of the presence of God and his tender love.

The contrast between this prayer meeting and the outside world is startling. All these teenagers live in suburban New York, with its feverish pace. The common high in suburban teenage life today is alcohol or marijuana, anything to escape from the dull monotony of a life without meaning. Whole families are caught up in this confusion. We see what we term good homes being torn apart, enmeshed in trouble and pain. Family relationships have broken down, and unity within family life has, for many, given way to a spirit of hopelessness. Some members of families "cannot stand" each other and "can't wait to get away" from each other.

However all this is resulting in a growing hunger for God and spiritual things. More and more people are returning to God. We are realizing that young people need the full gospel message, not a watered-down version of it. Many of them have been denied the challenge of the gospel; yet they hunger for God and desire to experience him. Members of our teen prayer group speak of Jesus as a friend, who accepts them and loves them just the way they are.

Our parish teenage prayer group began to meet at the end of 1972. About 75 to 100 teens meet every Thursday evening to pray. The teachings and testimonies they share at the prayer meetings are often surprising in their depth and maturity. They share their joys and troubles within this family of oneness. They realize that without God life has no meaning: "I am the vine, you are the branches. He who lives in me and I in him will produce abundantly, for apart from me you can do nothing" (John 15:5,NAB).

Here a teenager can be himself in the presence of Jesus and his friends. It is Jesus gently knocking on the hearts of the teens who gladly make room for him. One can rightly get a glimpse of their young hearts open to God's love. They pour out their pain, loneliness, frustrations, joys, hopes, and the rest. The most wonderful happening is that they allow Jesus to heal their hearts.

This openness to the Holy Spirit often reveals a wisdom that many parents do not have. In fact some of our teens have been God's instruments in bringing their parents back to the sacraments and closer to God. There is such a hunger in our society for true, open fellowship; for a genuine family spirit. This need is being met at the prayer meetings and in various other ministries within our parish.

Older teens lead the prayer meeting with order and spontaneity. There is present a true spirit of freedom and peace which only the Holy Spirit can bring. Having a mature young man lead the prayer meeting is most effective, as teens relate better to one close to their age. As at the adult prayer meeting, the teens have their own music group. The songs are chosen in the Spirit to express the theme of the prayer meeting and to suit the age group.

Our teenagers conduct Life in the Spirit seminars which have been adapted to their age level. They have "deepening talks," which are teachings on basic Christian living, growth in prayer, and other subjects. The seminars and teachings are conducted by the more mature members of the teen prayer group.

Like the adult prayer group they have a core group of dedicated teens who meet weekly to pray for the teen prayer meeting and to seek the Lord's guidance for the teen group. Members of this teen core group report, in turn, to the adult pastoral team. This team is composed of five adult prayer group members who, with myself, are the overall leaders of the parish prayer groups. This helps to bring order and unity into the community.

(In addition to the teen and adult prayer groups, we have prayer meetings at a local nursing home and at an apartment complex for senior citizens. We also have a prayer meeting for children, one for mothers of pre-school children, and one for married couples, besides a number of other in-home weekly prayer meetings. We take part, too, in a weekly prayer meeting at the county jail, as well as in visiting and praying with hospital patients. We have taken our motto for the parish prayer groups from Cardinal Suenens' first Malines Document: "To renew the whole of Christian life through the power of the Spirit under the lordship of Jesus.")

The teen prayer group is an important part of our parish renewal. The teens are the church of tomorrow. Growing in God's love, they have been filled with the desire to be of service to their families and the parish. They now give witness to Jesus in their homes, in their schools, in their daily lives. They minister to each other in prayer. They have given presentations on the work of Jesus in their lives to our parish and, by invitation, to outside parishes. Some of them take part in smaller prayer meetings in their schools. They plan weekend retreats a few times a year when they go to a retreat house to be refreshed and renewed. They plan picnics and outings, all contributing to a healthy, balanced life. Once a month they celebrate a special eucharistic liturgy for teens, as part of their regular prayer meeting.

Looking back over the past five years, I see the great blessing our teen prayer group has been to our parish. So many have attended the meetings over the years. Some are now married and part of the adult prayer group; others have gone away to college and jobs. Last year one entered the seminary to study for the priesthood.

The teens in our prayer group inspire hope within a society that badly needs it. I see them growing in God's love. I see a hunger and reverence for the eucharist, a growing love for Mary, growth in prayer, a thirst for Scripture as the living word of God, and a greater love for their families and their community. They are calling each other to holiness. "Blessed be the Lord the God of Israel because he has visited and ransomed his people" (Luke 1:68).

CHAPTER TWENTY-ONE

DAYTIME SHARING GROUPS
FOR WOMEN

Mary Mauren

B y this love you have for one another, everyone will know that you are my disciples" (John 13:35, *JB*). We all recognize that love for another is more than feeling, or even decision. It is the "washing feet" relationship to which Christians are called.

About three years ago, the leaders of our women's daytime prayer group began to realize that the large attendance at our prayer meetings kept us from knowing and loving each individual in this personal, serving way. The author of Hebrews exhorts, "Let love for your fellow believers continue and be a fixed practice with you—never let it fail" (Heb. 13:1, *Amplified Bible*). Even though our group had been in existence for about three years, we still needed a way to let our love become a "fixed practice." This led us to subdivide the large group into small fellowship or sharing groups. Our goal was to provide a relaxed time—apart from the weekly prayer meeting—for small groups of women to better know, love, and serve each other by sharing joys, sorrows, and deep needs with a few trusted friends.

We first tried forming groups of women according to the choices of the pastoral team members, each of whom was to serve as a group leader. Later, we tried rearranging the sharing groups according to the most recent Life in the Spirit Seminar, but eventually we discontinued this model as well. Our present groupings are based on geographical location, and we find the resultant variety within groups to be beneficial. (Grouping according to maturity in the Spirit might work well for some larger groups, and should be seriously considered. There is also merit in creating groups based on age or similar interests, such as all young mothers or older widows.) At the present time we have four groups.

Our biggest challenge, however, has not been figuring out how to divide the groups, but how to best enable each group to function in the Lord's way. We came to recognize that for any of our groups to operate smoothly, direction and leadership was needed.

Therefore, the pastoral team commissioned co-leaders for each group. Co-leaders work together under one member of the prayer group's pastoral team who has been given responsibility for this area. Originally, we expected each woman already on the pastoral team to help lead a sharing group, but this proved to be an unrealistic expectation: some were unequipped for it, others already over-committed.

We offered written guidelines for leading the groups. Some group leaders initially reacted negatively to this; they felt it would "quench the Spirit" to begin with any preconceived order or method. Experience has shown, however, that the guidelines actually result in *freeing* the Spirit to work more effectively. We have agreed, too, that the guidelines are a base from which to improvise or improve, according to each group's needs or limitations.

These are the guidelines our group leaders have found to be most helpful:

— Contact each member individually regarding upcoming meetings. This gives a chance to privately discuss any concerns, needs, and so on. When contacting new members, explain that it is a time exclusively for adults. Suggest trading babysitting with a member of another group, so that everyone can be truly present at her own meeting. Since the meetings aren't just social events, we don't give a general invitation at prayer meetings. Rather, we wait until a woman seems serious about her commitment to the prayer group and then invite her personally.

— Pray before your meeting — ideally, with your co-leader.

— When all are assembled, set the context of the meeting, remembering the goal of coming to know, love, and serve one another in a deeper way. Remind them that the meeting will end with prayer for each other. Ask everyone to help be responsible to end the meeting on time (about two and a half hours seems to work best). Begin with a brief time of song and praise.

— Remind the group of some simple guidelines for sharing (or introduce the concepts, if you have new people). The purpose is to glorify God and build each other up through sharing that doesn't reveal confidences or slip into gossip.

— Lovingly do whatever is necessary to keep the sharing focused on godly fellowship. Ask the Lord for wisdom and gentle firmness to draw out the reserved and deter the talkative, so that all feel included.

— Save time for intercessory prayer at the end. Try to reserve at least 30 minutes to pray for each other, ideally with the laying on of hands. A prayer circle might work best for some groups, with each woman leading the prayer for the one next to her, and the others adding as they feel led.

— Have eating enhance rather than detract from sharing time. We recommend brown-bag lunches or simple coffee times rather than potlucks or luncheons.

— After the gathering, evaluate the meeting's effectiveness with your co-leader. Pray and discuss problems, needs, and successes.

Over the years, groups have had some problems to work out. One that occurs frequently is unequal sharing. Too-verbal leaders, as well as individual members, sometimes dominate the meeting. It's hard to deal with compulsive talkers who show such a need to be heard. Yet it is obviously a disservice to consistently devote the greatest part of any group sharing time to one individual. Leaders should intervene gently, with a word or a touch, and steer the discussion into other areas. In some cases it is helpful to speak to individuals privately about their talkativeness.

Another problem is drawing out the shy. Some groups pick one member each meeting—starting with the quieter ones—and ask her to tell her life story. Hearing about parents, childhood, and growing-up years often gives a significant insight into a person previously known only in her adult role, and also helps focus on the least-heard-from members of the group.

Size is an important consideration. We've found eight to ten members to be ideal. Though bigger or smaller groups can work it's a fact that the larger the group, the harder it is to develop deep relationships.

The frequency of meetings is determined by individual situations. For many members of our prayer group, which holds its weekly prayer meetings during the daytime, an additional weekly daytime meeting would be a problem. For us, monthly meetings work best; for large parish prayer groups that meet in the evening, weekly sharing group meetings probably would be more helpful.

It is also important to be sensitive regarding the meeting place. Leaders need to encourage members to be candid about home availability and suitability. If a husband is not supportive of his wife's involvement in the charismatic renewal, it's usually best not to have the meeting at that home. When rotating homes, it's important to avoid the subtle pressure of comparing homemaking skills. Keep the meeting focused on Christian fellowship, rather than getting sidetracked by home tours or decorating tips and problems.

Remember that most problems that groups might have *are* manageable. Problems can be growth events, if the pairs of leaders learn to regularly evaluate the sessions. Healthy communication regarding the group's—and each other's—strengths and weaknesses is vital. The most effective base for working out group weaknesses is a loving relationship between the leaders, built on prayer and real communication.

Our four groups continue to be a real support to about 40 women who've come to know, love, and serve each other in a deeper Christian way. We support each other in prayer and phone conversations between meetings. We've learned it's more effective to channel our response to one another's needs—whether for transportation, family problems, bereavement or distress — through the small fellowship groups instead of the large prayer group.

Some husbands have repaired cars, offered transportation, or volunteered financial assistance. The support, and even involvement, of husbands who are not part of the charismatic renewal has been one of the most rewarding bonuses of the deepened relationships between us. It's a result, we believe, of our prayer and our commitment to support one another in becoming whole and loving persons, wives, mothers, and friends. As the group members' relationships developed, we began having small social events to which husbands were invited. Potlucks, bowling, home pizza, and sing-along sessions proved to be non-threatening, fun ways to get to know each other's spouses.

We know we still have a long way to go before we love and "wash feet" the way Jesus did. But we've set our hearts on the ideal of so loving and serving each other that everyone will know we belong to Jesus. Our goal is to lead others to say, "See how they love one another."

CHAPTER TWENTY-TWO

BOOK MINISTRY

John Boughton

Books are tools that can help people grow in Christian life, and one of the best services a prayer group can provide for its members is a book ministry that can help people find the right tools when they need them. The aim of every book ministry, no matter how small, should be to provide its customers with the very best materials.

Finances, space, and the number of people to be served will determine the *number* of titles; pastoral judgment must play a part in selecting the *appropriate* titles. A small book table should start out with the most basic materials and expand its selection as time goes on, according to the interests and needs of the particular prayer group it serves.

Many people who come to a book table have only a vague idea of what they want. They browse through the books on display and wait for something to catch their eye. Often, if a person they trust recommends a particular book, they will buy it; that is why many book jackets carry an endorsement from some well-known person. In a prayer group, people often rely on the judgment of the book-ministry worker. They trust him or her to know the literature. Recommending books is thus an important part of the bookseller's service.

In order to help people make their selections, the bookseller must know the books that he recommends. If possible, the bookseller should read every book offered at the table. If he can't do that, he can usually get an adequate idea of a book's content by skimming through it at a moderate pace. If skimming is impossible, he should have another person read the books and write a brief synopsis of each.

When helping a person find the right book, it is best to begin by asking him or her what he or she has read and is interested in. If the person is new to the charismatic renewal, he should start by reading the basic books. The latest best-seller may be *Husbands, Wives, Parents, Children,* but something such as *The Cross and the Switchblade* would be more useful to a new person.

One way the bookseller can serve his customers is by helping them balance their reading selections. Many people tend to read only one type of book, neglecting equally valuable books in another style. If someone has been concentrating only on serious theological books, the book-table worker might recommend something in a different vein, perhaps a testimony such as *The Hiding Place.*

The book-ministry worker can expect that the Lord will give him the inspiration and direction he needs to guide people to the right books. The Spirit of God should be as actively involved in book ministry as in every other part of the body.

Besides fostering Christian life in individuals, a book can supplement the Lord's work in the entire prayer group. The bookseller can contribute a great deal to the prayer group by recommending the right book at the right time. Recommendations of this sort should not be made too often; otherwise, people may become burdened with a backlog of unread books. It is best for the bookseller to note when the Lord is speaking clearly to the group about a particular topic, and then recommend one exceptionally good book in the area. He should be sure to consult the prayer group leaders before making his recommendation.

A book ministry will accomplish little if the prayer group is not aware of the services and materials it provides. A general announcement will help alert people, especially newcomers, to the book table's location. Such an announcement should be fairly simple, and can be included with other announcements at the beginning or end of the meeting.

Since the workers at the book table can't help every person who stops to browse, it's important that the materials be displayed in a way that will help people find what they're looking for. The bookseller can learn much in this area from commercial marketing techniques, though he should remember that his basic purpose is not to sell books but to help people find a deeper life with the Lord.

The book table should be placed in the room where the prayer meeting is held; preferably, along a wall near the main exit where people will see it as they pass in and out. There should be sufficient space around the table for people to gather without blocking the exit. Most people will stop at the book table after the prayer meeting, and several workers may be needed to serve them adequately. Before the prayer meeting, the table is usually less busy.

The book table should be identified with a sign on the wall above and behind it. The books on the table should be grouped into categories, each category identified with its own sign. This is especially important if the book ministry is large enough to use several tables. Signs can indicate sections such as "personal testimony," "introductory," "personal growth," "spiritual gifts," "prayer," "marriage and family." Sections of the table devoted to magazines or to records may not need signs since those materials create their own visual display.

A prayer meeting book table *is* a business, no matter how small or unbusinesslike it may seem. The Lord wants his people to be open and forthright in business matters and offer a good witness to the business world. This has an important bearing on how the book ministry presents itself to the local bank, the state sales-tax agency, the Internal Revenue Service, and the various dealers who supply it with merchandise and materials. The book ministry should be set up according to the normal expectations of these agencies. It is very important, for instance, to pay suppliers' bills when due. It is important to keep reliable records for the bank and for tax agencies.

A checking account is essential to any business. It provides a convenient means of paying bills by mail and keeping legal receipts. It also eliminates the need to keep a great deal of cash on hand. The book-ministry account should be separate from the personal account of the bookseller. Separate accounts will prevent commingling of business and personal funds.

A book ministry is likely to make some profit, since it has so few expenses beyond the cost of merchandise. The profits can be used to support other needs in the prayer group, to provide books for people who can't afford to pay, or to reduce selling prices. Other possible uses include a lending library of books and cassettes, or an expansion of the book-table inventory. When inventory grows, it takes more money to pay current invoices, which are usually due within 30 days of the shipping date. If sales are not increasing as fast as inventory, it may be necessary to use profits simply to get the invoices paid on time.

A prayer group may incorporate as a nonprofit religious organization and receive an exemption from paying taxes on its income, including the profits from booktable sales. (The group may also obtain a status which will allow it to receive contributions that donors may deduct from their taxes.) Prayer groups who want further information on incorporation should consult a competent attorney.

If the prayer group is not incorporated, the book table is, legally, a *proprietorship* owned by some person, usually the person running the book ministry. Business income, expenses, and profit or loss must be attributed to the owner's private income for internal revenue purposes. A simple accounting system will be needed for a reliable record of profit and loss.

The basic accounting record is the checkbook. All money collected at the book table, except some fixed amount kept as a change fund, should be promptly deposited in the book-ministry account. And when the bookseller pays bills from various suppliers, he should always use checks from the account. The book ministry should never pay out cash, only checks. Every deposit into the book-ministry account, and every check written from the checkbook, must be entered in the checkbook record just as if it were a personal checkbook. Each entry must be dated and clearly described.

After a bill has been paid it should be marked with the number of the check used for payment and filed away.

A book ministry operates to serve a prayer group rather than to make a profit. Therefore its accounting system need not be concerned with elaborate accounts and reports. It should simply record the activities of the book-ministry funds. A simple, monthly report provides sufficient information for government tax agencies and for those in the prayer group who are responsible for the book ministry.

Most states require a sales-tax license for all merchandise sold at retail. The individual "owner" or the prayer group as a corporation should apply to the state for this retail sales-tax license. If the business has been operating without a license, there may be back taxes or even penalties to pay. It is advisable to get the sales-tax license and set things up legally from the beginning.

Despite the apparently confusing array of business-related considerations, starting up and maintaining an effective book ministry in the prayer group is not difficult, and the service it can provide to individuals and the group as a whole makes it most worthwhile.

CHAPTER TWENTY-THREE

SING TO THE LORD
A LEGAL SONG

Donna Kelly

JOYFUL, expressive music has become a hallmark of the charismatic renewal. Singing is an important part of worship for most prayer groups and, not surprisingly, most groups use some kind of songbook — often homemade — to help people learn the songs and join in the singing.

But there's more to making songbooks than meets the eye. Most people are unaware of the regulations that must be followed. Suppose your prayer group wanted to publish its own songbook for use at the weekly prayer meeting. How would you go about it?

The first step, at least, is relatively simple: pick the songs you want to print. Pick songs that are popular and will be used often, or else you'll be wasting time, energy, and money. Be sure that the lyrics are appropriate — in keeping with Christian teaching, not overly introspective or sentimental — and that the melody isn't too difficult for people to learn and sing easily. Above all, expect the Lord to guide you in selecting the songs that will be most helpful to your group.

So far, so good. But from here on, things get complicated. It's unfortunate, but many of the informal songbooks used by prayer groups are illegal: they are printed in violation of the copyright law, which protects the legitimate rights of authors, composers, arrangers, and publishers. Many people don't realize that most songs are *owned* by someone, and that the owner has the right to determine how his property may be used. Before you can print someone else's song, even if it's only for private use on a small scale, you *must* get his permission. That's the law.

So, after you've decided you want to use a particular song, you have to find out who owns it. The easiest way to do this is to look through existing songbooks and check the credits and copyright notations for the song you're interested in; church and school musicians in your area should be able to help you with this. There are also other sources of information: books listing popular religious songs, professional music agencies, and publishing companies. As a last resort, you can contact the Copyright Office itself, in Washington, D.C.

Some songs are in the public domain, that is, no one owns legal rights to them and they may be published without obtaining permission. However, very few of the songs popular in the charismatic renewal are in this category. Never assume that a song is in the public domain without verifying it. Always look for a copyright owner before printing.

Once you've determined who owns a song (usually a publishing company) you have to write and ask permission to print it. Describe your intended project fully and completely. The publisher will want to know who you are and what kind of book you're printing: a songbook for long-term use, for example, or a program for one-time use, such as a wedding booklet. Tell him how many copies you want to make, whether you want words only or the full musical arrangement, and whether you intend to sell the finished product. Let him know how soon you need to hear from him, but allow at least six to eight weeks.

Your request will be answered in writing. The publisher is entirely free to grant or refuse permission, or to impose certain conditions on the use of his property. Most publishers will require proof that the song has been printed accurately, with correct credits and copyright notice. Most will also charge a fee: 2¢ per song per copy is average, though rates range between ½¢ and 4¢

per reprint. A publisher may refuse permission to reprint his material; that is his prerogative. If a polite letter requesting reconsideration doesn't help, then the matter is closed and you may not print the song.

If one of the songs you want to print has never been published before — for example, if you want to print a song written by someone in your group — you need to take special care. The composer can actually lose legal ownership of his creation. If a new song is published without proper copyright notification it goes into the public domain, and the author loses his rights to it.

Unpublished manuscripts of new songs should be labeled "For confidential use only. Not for circulation, distribution, or publication. All rights in this work are the property of (author's name)," or words to that effect. When the song is first officially published, it must bear the proper copyright notice: "© (copyright owners' name) 1977" is usually sufficient.

As a rule of thumb, for a large songbook (50 or more songs), allow at least six months for the process of securing permissions, and don't start printing until you have signed licenses for *all* the songs. Incidentally, the various translations of the Bible, as well as the official liturgical texts of churches — such as the *Lectionary for Mass* and the *Book of Common Prayer* also are protected by copyright.

Whether you choose to print your songbook on the church mimeo machine or have it done by a local printing shop, there are a few things to bear in mind. Make each page accurate and as legible as possible. Use either song numbers or page numbers, but not both: it confuses people. Make certain you print the credits and copyright notices *exactly* the way the copyright owners want them. Somewhere in the book, print a notice that you'll be glad to correct any errors in future editions. Though not all publishers require it, it's a nice gesture to send a copy of the book as soon as it's been printed.

Finally, don't forget to pay your royalties! Some arrangement for this will have been made in your agreement with the publisher; the easiest way is to pay upon the printing of the book. Many prayer groups find it helpful to open a special checking account, in the name either of the group or of the songbook itself.

Have members donate money to the account, and use it to pay all the bills.

Obviously, making your own songbook is not a simple matter. For most groups it will be far easier, and much more economical, to purchase a ready-made songbook (you can always add one or two of your own favorite songs later—legally, of course). If you decide to print your own book, remember that it is *your* responsibility to locate copyright owners, obtain reprint permission, and follow all guidelines and regulations.

Authors, composers, arrangers, and publishers make their living by making their music available to the public. By using their property without their permission, you deprive them of their livelihood and you break the law. Lawsuits can be brought against violators of the copyright laws, including prayer groups and churches, by copyright owners or by the government. Fines can include lump-sum damage payments, per-copy charges, and court costs. It's much easier and far more righteous to do it correctly from the start.

CHAPTER TWENTY-FOUR

DIAL A PRAY-ER

Bobbie Cavnar

A BOUT five years ago, our community began to feel a need for a way to inform one another, on short notice, of urgent prayer requests. We had a number of expectant mothers at the time, and we all felt a strong desire to support them in prayer during the birth of their children. To communicate quickly and effectively, we devised a simple telephone system, in which each person in the community is responsible for contacting two or three other people whenever there is an urgent prayer request

The leader of the community sets things in motion by calling the people assigned to him. They, in turn, phone the people they are responsible for, and so on. Each person, immediately after making his phone calls, gathers together his family or household and, regardless of the time of day or night, they pray for the situation. In most cases the entire community — more than a thousand people — can be contacted and at prayer in as little as ten minutes.

We publish the phone assignments on a chart that looks something like a backward sports tournament chart, starting with one person and fanning out to encompass the entire community.

Thus, anyone can see at a glance who he is responsible for calling, and who is responsible for calling *him*. Whenever someone can't reach one of his assigned people, he must make that person's calls for him, so that the progression will continue.

Of course, the more people that can be reached and told to start praying, the more effective is the system. For this reason, we normally start the "prayer line" during the dinner hour or, perhaps, at around ten in the evening — times when we know most people will be home. We have found that in most cases we can be somewhat flexible as to when to start the process; for example, situations that arise during the night can usually wait until morning. But when a situation is truly critical and cannot wait, we start the process regardless of the time, day or night, and contact as many people as possible so that the maximum prayer power can be brought to bear.

We've had some dramatic examples of how effective this kind of prayer can be. Late one night, I was awakened by a phone call from a man in the community, who said his expectant wife had just been admitted to the maternity ward and was due to deliver her baby at any time. We'd already had one other prayer request on the prayer line that night, and I was kind of tired, so instead of getting everybody at my house out of bed I just made my three calls, said a quick prayer, and went back to sleep. This was about one o'clock in the morning.

At about seven, I got another call from the husband: "Bobbie, didn't you start the prayer line? My wife's labor is stalled and nothing's happening!" Evidently, everybody else had done the same thing I had — made their calls and gone back to sleep! I started the process again — reminding everyone to pray more vigorously this time — and thirty-five minutes later the baby was born.

Another time, I got a phone call at about nine in the evening from a woman who said her nine-year-old boy had apparently gotten lost at the Texas State Fair. This particular day had been set aside especially for school children, and there were more than 30,000 of them on the fairgrounds. Her son was supposed to have come to a contact point at five o'clock to meet his ride home, but had not shown up.

One of our community's elders went over to the woman's home to talk with her and see what the situation was. The police had already arrived, and things were beginning to look grim. It seemed clear that the boy definitely was lost, and we decided to activate the prayer line. I made the first phone call at about eleven, and less than twenty minutes after we started praying the police found the boy.

Precisely because this system is so effective, it's important to make sure that it's used in an orderly way. We've found that it seems to invite certain kinds of abuse, and we've learned ways to avoid the most common problems.

It's vital that everyone understand what kinds of prayer requests should and should not be transmitted. We use the prayer line only for serious problems that truly require the prayer of the entire community: a lost child, for example, or a serious accident. Even in these cases, we activate it only when we're sure the problem actually exists—that is, not on the basis of second-hand or hearsay information ("So-and-so just told me that so-and-so said that such-and-such happened"), and not when it's still too early to tell if, say, the child really *is* lost.

The system is always implemented in support of expectant mothers in the community when they go to the hospital, day or night. Even though childbirth is not usually a life-or-death situation, we consider it a special opportunity to love and support one another. We also use the system to notify community members of important announcements, such as cancellations of community-wide meetings, when time is short and there's no other way to spread the news.

As for more long-range problems, such as troubled marriages or problems with teenagers: we encourage people to pray for these things regularly, but we don't activate the prayer line for them.

It's also important that people understand clearly who we will pray for in this way. We implement the system only on behalf of committed members of the community. We specifically do not implement it for friends, relatives, acquaintances, people who have come to one or two prayer meetings, and so on. When we began using this system, it was not uncommon to receive telephone requests from total strangers, asking the community to pray for someone. The system rapidly became ineffective: people simply don't respond when they've been awakened two or three times in one night to pray for persons or situations they know nothing about. Again, we encourage individual community members to pray for these needs, but we don't activate the prayer line for them.

The key to a successful prayer line is commitment. People have to make a definite commitment to be part of the process — to say, "Yes, you can call me in the middle of the night, and I'll make my three calls and I'll get up and pray for whatever the problem is." This becomes especially important in prayer groups. In our case, participating in the system is simply part of a person's basic commitment to the community. A prayer group would need to be very clear on who is participating and who isn't, on who is in charge (in our community, only one person has the authority to start the process — otherwise, we found, things rapidly get out of control), and on what the ground rules are. People have to commit themselves to respecting that authority and following the ground rules.

In the context of this kind of commitment, such a system of intercessory prayer can be very effective. We've used it many times in the past five years, and the Lord has always been faithful about answering us. There is tremendous power when the body of Christ joins together in prayer!

CHAPTER TWENTY-FIVE

PRAYER GROUPS
IN THE MASTER'S PLAN

Gerry Rauch

SOMETIMES we hear the plea, "If there is a God, why doesn't he make a difference in the world?" If the question is sincere, it can be a very good question indeed, largely because it's *not* clear that he makes a difference in the lives of Christians. Many Christians' experience of Christianity is limited to hearing about Jesus, intellectually accepting the truth of the story, and then attempting to act consistently with it. They can point to the New Testament words that Jesus is "the word of life made manifest *and we saw it*" (1 John 1:2), but often they cannot testify the same themselves.

But something new is happening in the charismatic renewal. When we were baptized in the Spirit, we experienced a God who does make a difference. Instead of being limited to the intellectual assent that the Holy Spirit has been given to us, we experience him living in us and acting in us. Personal contact with the Lord becomes a daily experience, the Bible becomes a book of power that changes lives, people are healed and freed, evangelism works. In short, we see "the word of life made manifest."

But it doesn't stop there. The revelation of Jesus—his words, his actions—is not just a bunch of separate fragments cast out for

the winds to carry wherever chance leads them. There is a plan to
this revelation; it builds up to something. God is not manifesting
himself in a random or chaotic way with no ultimate purpose.
Just as it is inadequate to make Christianity a new humanism in
which God does not act, it is inadequate to receive the Lord's
words and actions without letting them lead us to the ultimate
purpose God has in mind for them.

St. Paul gives the most direct statement of God's ultimate goal:
"He has made known to us...the mystery of his will, according to
his purpose which he set forth in Christ as a plan for the fullness
of time, *to unite all things in him*, things in heaven and things on
earth....that he might create in himself *one new man*" (Eph.
1:10, 2:15, *RSV*). There are other images in the New Testament
for the same reality: the body of Christ, the bride of Christ, the
new temple, the new Israel, and so on. All of them indicate that
God's purpose in manifesting himself to mankind is to create a
corporate reality made up of Christians in union with Christ.

"The word of life made manifest" is ultimately, then, this single
corporate reality: the one new man. We have inherited such a
strong individualism in our Christianity that we frequently have
a hard time seeing this corporate purpose of God. We tend to
think of Christianity in terms of individual saints and personal
plans for spiritual growth. Corporate ways of thinking are
unfamiliar to us, and we tend to overlook them. We perhaps
think that this unity is reserved for heaven.

But the Lord himself prayed that we would experience unity
now: "That they may all be one...so that the world may believe
that thou hast sent me" (John 17:21). God wants to manifest
himself in the world, and the ultimate focus of his revelation is
the one, united new man. If the world can ask that God make a
difference, it can also validly ask that Christianity make a visible
difference in the lives of Christians by their unity with one
another.

Even in the charismatic renewal, the heritage of individual
Christianity that we have received can make us stop at the level of
the presence and power of God in the baptism of the Holy Spirit
and the spiritual gifts. We can fail to see the necessity of their
focusing on the full manifestation of the body of Christ.

Once a guest came to my home, a leader in the charismatic renewal from another area. He was concerned about an accusation that was being made against the prayer groups in his area, namely, that they were overemphasizing the spiritual gifts.

As I spent time with him I began to get the picture of the renewal in his area. The leaders couldn't work together well. Any group that existed for a while eventually split into smaller ones. Some groups were no longer attracting new members, and most groups that were couldn't hold them for long.

A little later, he returned to the accusation about overemphasizing spiritual gifts and asked me how he could respond to it. What I had to tell him was, "You *are* overemphasizing spiritual gifts. Look at the state of things: your groups keep splitting, the leaders can't agree among themselves or work together. You should stop paying so much attention to the spiritual gifts and learn other things, like loving one another in a committed way and working together."

Plunging into the charismatic renewal without building the unity the Lord wants amounts to an overemphasis on spiritual gifts, having the members without the body. To put it another way: Without the end product in mind, the manifestation of the spiritual gifts will be misguided.

One of the New Testament images for God's people is the new temple. "You are fellow citizens with the saints...joined together...into a temple in the Lord" (Eph. 2:19, 21). This is a strongly corporate image, but we have a hard time understanding it.

Consider this story. An architect set out to construct a temple. First, he gathered the stones with which he planned to build. Now, this architect had an uncanny ability to select just the right stones. Where others would overlook a stone, he would clean it and cut it to enhance its beauty and strength.

When he had gathered the stones he wanted, it was a magnificent collection. People came from miles around to admire it. In fact so many people came that the architect changed his mind about building a temple; instead, he built a museum to house his stone collection. And it became very popular.

God is not like the architect. He hasn't changed his plan that was "hidden for ages" (Eph. 3:9). But *we* tend to think like the architect. We see individual Christians more than the new corporate reality that God wants to make of them. Even when we use the word "fellowship," we tend to have an image more like that rock museum where all the beautiful new stones are gathered, than like a temple where each stone has been fitted into place and built together with the others so that a new corporate reality can exist: the new temple.

As we work within the charismatic renewal, let us ask ourselves what God has in mind. We want to build the way he wants us to, toward the goal of uniting all things in Christ. What can we do?

First, we can pray for unity. Then we can tackle some practical issues within our groups: right relationships, committed love, wisdom for working and seeking the Lord together. And then we can start working toward unity with other groups.

If it is time for our group to make progress in any of these areas, it is of prime importance that we seek help from existing groups or communities that have already experienced what we are still learning. It is hard for a group or community to grow on its own, just as it is hard for an individual Christian to grow on his own.

From its inception the charismatic renewal has been about the manifestation of the Lord and his life, about a God who makes a difference in the world. For the renewal to mature, it has to advance toward that ultimate plan of God, the unity of everything in the one new man, Jesus Christ.

CONTRIBUTORS

Larry Alberts is a coordinator of the Servants of the Lord, a Christian community in Minneapolis, Minnesota.

John Blattner is managing editor of *New Covenant* magazine. He has served as leader in several prayer groups and is currently a leader in The Word of God, a Christian community in Ann Arbor, Michigan.

John Boughton is distribution manager for Charismatic Renewal Services in South Bend, Indiana.

Jim Brassil is pastor of Our Lady of Mercy parish in Hicksville, New York.

Jack Brombach is a coordinator of the Servants of the Lord.

Bobbie Cavnar is a leader of The Christian Community of God's Delight in Dallas, Texas.

Jim Cavnar is the author of *Participating in Prayer Meetings*. He is a coordinator of The Word of God.

Randy Cirner is a coordinator of The Word of God.

Father Bob Duggan is director of the Detroit Catholic Charismatic Renewal Coordinating Center in Detroit, Michigan.

John Evans is a leader of the People of Joy Covenant Community in Phoenix, Arizona.

Donna Kelly is the publications editor for Servant Music in Ann Arbor, Michigan.

Father George Kosicki is coordinator of Bethany House of Intercession in Warwick, Rhode Island.

Hal Langevin is a coordinator of the Servants of the Lord.

Mary Mauren is a leader of Agape, a women's daytime prayer group in the Seattle, Washington area.

Gabe Meyer is a coordinator of the City of the Angels, a Christian community in Los Angeles, California.

Kevin Perrotta is an associate editor of *New Covenant* and a leader in The Word of God.

David Podegracz is a coordinator of the City of the Angels.

Gerry Rauch is a coordinator of The Word of God.

Jim Rolland is a coordinator of the Servants of the Lord. He is responsible for the community's music group.

Father Michael Scanlan is president of the College of Steubenville in Steubenville, Ohio.

Sister Ann Thérèse Shields is director of the Office for National Charismatic Ministries at the College of Steubenville in Steubenville, Ohio. She is a contributing editor of *New Covenant*.

Bruce Yocum is a coordinator of The Word of God.